women together

women together

portraits of love, commitment, and life

Essays by Mona Holmlund   Photographs by Cyndy Warwick

Foreword by Candace Gingrich

RUNNING PRESS

PHILADELPHIA · LONDON

Text © 1999 by Mona Holmlund

Photographs © 1999 by Cyndy Warwick

© 1999 by Running Press

Printed in China

9   8   7   6   5   4   3   2   1
Digit on the right indicates the number of this printing

Library of Congress Cataloging-in-Publication Number 97-66832

ISBN 0-7624-0064-1

Typography: Bell Gothic and Perpetua

This book may be ordered by mail from the publisher. Please include $2.50 for postage and handling.
But try your bookstore first!

Running Press Book Publishers

125 South Twenty-second Street

Philadelphia, Pennsylvania 19103-4399

Visit us on the web!

www.runningpress.com

For all who read these pages, that hearts may be moved and minds opened,
in the spirit of the One who made and loves us all.

—MH

To the inner courage that is necessary for a woman
to openly love another woman.

—CW

acknowledgments

An incalculable debt is owed to all the women, some of whom do not appear in these pages, who generously welcomed me
into their homes and lives. The meals, conversation, and friendship we shared have been the most memorable parts of this experience.
Even more than making this book possible, you have changed my way of looking at the world.

Thanks also to the various people who envisioned this project and brought it to fruition — in particular, Cyndy Warwick
for thinking of me in the first place and for her continuing friendship, Tara Ann McFadden for all her hard work at the beginning, and especially
Patty Smith for being such a gifted and intelligent editor as well as a pleasure to work and laugh with. Special thanks to Bob
for his enthusiasm, on-going friendship, and encouragment to play — which helped me to work.

And most of all, I can only begin to express the overwhelming gratitude I feel to my parents, Patricia and Blaine,
whose unconditional love and support have always made it possible for me to follow my bliss; to my sister, Cheryl, who showed me that love is selfless;
and to Richard, who read every word of every draft and in doing so taught me to believe what he had always said — love is extending yourself.

— MH

I'd like to thank all the people who helped put this project together. Although there are a lot of special people who put in an extra effort,
they are too numerous to thank individually, but my heartfelt appreciation goes out to each and every one of them
for their kindness and support — particularly the couples who participated in this book.

Thanks to Running Press for their willingness to take on such an important project and especially to Maria Lewis for being open to my vision.
John Giambrone, thank you for bringing this project to Mona and me. Mona Holmlund, thank you for your infinite patience, cooperation,
and trust in being my partner on this book. James Wilkens — you are the best, so selfless with me and so knowledgeable about photography.

Sheila Brown, I absolutely could not have done this without your assistance, support — and love. Grandma Marjorie, thank you for your passion
for photography — you have been my inspiration. Mom, I have accomplished everything in my life with your support and open arms.
Where would I be without you? Gurumayi Chidvilasananda, your benevolent grace has changed my life. With great respect and great love,
I thank you again, and again, and again. Sadgurunāth Mahārāj kī Jay!

— CW

Contents

foreword

THE WAY I TELL IT, I HAVE THREE COMING OUT stories: First, when I was about twenty, I came out to myself and acknowledged who I was. Then, about four months later I came out to my family. Finally, I came out to the nation.

I had been living a fairly politically innocent life in Harrisburg, Pennsylvania, working full-time at a golf store and loading trucks for UPS at night, when my brother Newt became Speaker of the House. It didn't take very long for a reporter to ask me if I was gay. I said, "Yes."

The reporter was from the Associated Press, so this wasn't just the "Weekly Shopper." My coming out was on the wire that night and was front-page news the next morning.

Soon the Human Rights Campaign asked me to become part of the "National Coming-Out Project." They wanted me to travel the country doing town-hall meetings and to talk about the importance of openness and honesty.

At the time, I really didn't know too much about the gay-rights movement. But I did know what the injustices were. I couldn't have lived with myself knowing there was an opportunity to do something, and I hadn't done it. Once again, I said, "Yes."

I haven't regretted a single moment. I would implode or spontaneously combust if I had to try to be a closeted person again. This conviction has particular resonance when I am part of a couple, and *Women Together* reinforces that belief. The publication of a book like this is an outing of sorts—but a joyful, celebratory one.

The women you will meet in the following pages have all had to make the same decision I have and have shared a similar journey. They have all said "yes!" to being out, but also to life and to love. I could never personally go back to a life that is repressed and fearful, and one of the rewards is being able to be part of open, honest, committed relationships. It has been important for me to be part of what I like to call "The Lesbian Visibility Project."

Like some of the couples in this book, I will walk down the street with my partner, holding hands, being myself. It is natural for us to want to hold hands and call each other "Honey." To try not to do that would be wrong. I do not feel intimidated by the people who see us or by what they might be thinking. Individuals have a tremendous power to change the perceptions of those around them. I think my being gay—and Newt Gingrich's sister—is an ironic thorn in the side of allies of the far Right who want everyone to believe that we come from families that aren't "normal"—where something has gone wrong, that gays are somehow a mistake.

This is what my work with HRC's National Coming-Out Project, what being out, and what a book like Women Together are all about— changing perceptions so we can change laws and end discrimination. Fighting prejudice and homophobia is a life-long struggle that we all share. Women Together is one advance in that battle. The goals are all the rights, all the responsibilities, all the benefits and privileges that non-gay people take for granted.

We need access to our partner's hospital room, the right to make decisions about her care, and legal recognition if something should happen to her. We need workplace protection; employment discrimination interferes with a basic human right—it affects people's ability to take care of themselves, and if they have a family, to feed, house, and clothe that family. Our children can even be taken away from us because the rights of the non-biological parent are not recognized. We can't even file taxes together.

You will see these struggles played out in the lives of the women in Women Together. One couple has fought through bureaucracy and achieved official recognition for their relationship from Canadian Immigration. Two other women are fighting for the right to legally marry in Hawaii. One couple is dealing with serious illness and the insecurity that brings. Another woman lost her job with the military. Still another couple is raising their children in a spirit of openness, actively educating those around them about gay families.

Ultimately, the battle is about families. It is about families being recognized as something more than the genders of the people involved. As the couples collected here can attest, families are families because of what is inside them; they are about love, security, and trust. As these women will tell you, to be continually told that our relationships are not valid is infuriating. To know that when politicians talk about the "American dream," they are not talking about us, that they are excluding millions of people—that is an outrage. All of the couples in Women Together see themselves as part of something "bigger than the both of them." Whether they call it a marriage, a family, or a partnership, the feelings they have for each other extend beyond them as separate individuals, uniting them with all people who have ever been in love.

Being out and being visible isn't simply "flaunting" our gayness. We should not be denied the right to be who we are and love who we choose. We have to be honest. We have to let people know how we feel about the way we are treated.

Until sexual orientation is not the reason that we are denied the same rights, responsibilities, and protections as non-gay people, it has to be an issue that is continually brought to everyone's attention. Ultimately I would like sexual orientation to be irrelevant, but as long as someone can fire me, or evict me, or beat me up walking home one night—just because I am gay, then my sexual orientation is very relevant. There are a lot of people out there who would feel able to be more open and honest about who they are if they didn't have to live under the specter of fear because of who they love.

Women Together takes lesbian couples out of that shadow and holds them up to the light in a spirit of celebration. These women rejoice in their love—and I invite you to join them. Because the relationships you will read about have been fought for, and have endured, in the face of such adversity, they should be cherished even more. *Women Together* is a positive representation of what lesbians can achieve. This perhaps is truly the ultimate goal: that all of us should have the right to have love in our lives in an open, honest, fulfilling, and joyful way.

—*Candace Gingrich*

introduction

*W*OMEN *TOGETHER* IS A CELEBRATION OF WOMEN
loving women, but the relationships you will read about
in the following pages are so diverse as to defy catego-
rization and easy analysis. Over the past three years we have traveled
from the Canadian Prairies to America's Heartland, from New York
to L.A., from Miami Beach to Puget Sound, from Alaska to Hawaii,
to find couples of different ages, races, and walks of life to share
their unique perspectives. We interviewed and photographed women
who have been together for more than thirty years, and women who
haven't even lived that long.

Still, even with all of this diversity, it is almost impossible to
present portraits of couples without reference to formal commitment—but with women together it is not so simple. Some couples
consider themselves married and call each other "Wife." Others prefer the phrase "commitment ceremony" and want nothing to do with
heterosexual conventions. While one couple is suing for the right to
legally marry, still another thinks the state should stay out of everyone's bedrooms. Some of these couples are not monogamous—though
they consider their commitment to be just as strong.

Apart from the tremendous variety within their relationships,
these couples also have widely different ways of relating to the rest of
the world. Some of the couples have children and spend most of their
time among families with straight parents. Some of these women
have had nothing to do with politics, or activism, or even other lesbian couples, while still others are completely immersed in gay
culture, as writers, lobbyists, or club owners. Some are committed to
what they see as the advantages of loving women; others say they
would love their partner "even if she were a man." Some are critical
of gay culture, while others identify with it completely.

What can we make of this bewildering array of opinions and life-
styles? It would seem that to say someone is part of a lesbian couple
is ultimately to say nothing at all—the only common denominator
being the gender of the lovers. However, all these women share much
in common. As women who love women, whether they accept the
label lesbian or not, they have all traveled a similar path to come to
the point where you will meet them in these pages, to the point where
they can be out and open about who they are and who they love.

There are women in this book whose earliest kindergarten
memories confirm for them that they are "different." It would
have been soul-destroying for these women to try to follow their

gender-proscribed path in our society. And there are still others who consciously chose not to blindly accept hand-me-down expectations. These are women who may have been married, who may have had children, who may have loved men. But all are women who now feel they have found something better. They are women who feel that they have, as one put it, "something that fits more for your soul than for your role." These are all women who have chosen to blaze their own path in life, flying in the face of convention against all expectations and much opposition. In this light it is not much of a stretch to understand homophobia as misogyny—that malignant anxiety that surrounds the ideas of what women can be, what they can do, and how they should behave. In opposition to that fearfulness, defiantly-out lesbians point the way toward a staggering freedom of choice, an overwhelming, mind-boggling, invigorating redefinition of identity and the wonderful, joyous freedom to really be, and know, yourself. What is a lesbian? She is anything she wants to be.

WHEN TWO WOMEN COME TOGETHER the possibilities are endless. You will hear these women talk about true equality, profound intimacy, and a sense of connection that goes beyond mere understanding. Clearly the questions need to be reformed. The issue is not who we love, but how. Perhaps lesbian relationships should be thought of differently: not that lesbians love women, but why; not that two women have formed a partnership, but what it really means to be a woman individually. Indeed, in these pages you will meet a diverse array of women and discover romances and relationships as varied as the individuals themselves. Ultimately, these are snapshots of the couples as we saw them at the time. *Women Together* is, in every sense, a collaborative effort. The images you will encounter and the words you will read are very much the voices and faces of these women as we saw them. It was their willingness to share so much with us, even when it was risky or discomforting, that made this book possible. We know that we have not done justice to the full complexity and nuance of even one of these relationships. Some believe they have found their soulmate and that special magic unites them for all time. Others think it is hard work and perseverance that guarantees longevity.

Ultimately, however, the common ground is far more substantial than the ephemeral differences. The one truth that unites all this chaotic diversity is its shared humanity. What memories do a couple in their seventies cherish when they recall their first glimpse of each other? What do two high school sweethearts anticipate on prom night? Love, commitment, faith, joy, sorrow . . . this is the stuff of life, which we all share—women, men, gay or straight.

Ideally the words and images of others can free us from the limiting isolation of our own point of view. In *Women Together*, you will be reassured by the familiar and challenged by the unexpected. You will find images of couples that will affirm your feelings about love and relationships and others that will inspire you to see things differently—to broaden your understanding of what it means to be a lesbian, to be a woman, to be a person in love.

It is our hope that taken as a whole *Women Together* will provide insight, understanding, and celebration of the love between women. Ideally it will demonstrate that love, in whatever guise, defies easy explanation. Love cannot be categorized, reduced, dismissed, or denied. It is resilient, continuous, unexpected, inviting joy and delight, evoking reverence and gratitude.

We offer this book as a gift to those who will be inspired, uplifted, and encouraged by it. And to those who venture to open their minds and hearts, we hope you will find in these pages the warmth, compassion, and understanding that love calls forth, because *Women Together* is, above all, a celebration of the magic, the mystery, and the power of love.

—*Mona Holmlund & Cyndy Warwick*

Chelle Mileur & Tina Podlodowski

"YOU'D THINK TWO WOMEN COULD PLAN THIS better," laughs Chelle Mileur.

Chelle was pregnant during Tina Podlodowski's campaign and due on election day. So, their joke was: if Tina won, they would call the baby Victoria; and if she lost, her name would be Louise.

At a candidate forum in a conservative area, an old man approached Tina and Chelle. He looked them both up and down, then gruffly pointed his cane at Chelle's burgeoning stomach and demanded of Tina, "Did you do that!?"

Tina thought, "Oh no, I don't need this," and steeled herself for a confrontation. She looked him squarely in the eye and said, "Yeah, I did."

"Well," he replied, "I guess I am going to vote for you then because if you can do that, you can do anything."

The campaign was in November 1995. Tina won the election. Now, she and Chelle are also the proud mothers of baby Grace, born on Thanksgiving.

Tina is a Seattle City Council member, and, not unusual in that city, she is also a Microsoft millionaire. Chelle was a computer consultant for twelve years, most recently at IBM, before she "retired to pursue the new career of being Grace's mom." Now they use their combined resources, financial and creative, to raise Grace and to raise consciousness about lesbian and gay families. They have established the Podlodowski/Mileur Fund to support projects that promote self-esteem and well-being for children from lesbian and gay families.

"Our focus is very specifically on making school safe for Grace. We don't want her to get called names because her parents are queer," explains Chelle. "We started in the schools because that is where Grace is going to spend most of her time in her formative years."

It is estimated that there are between six and fourteen million kids in America who have at least one gay parent. For the sake of those children, as well as their own, Chelle and Tina want to encourage a concept of family "defined as something that is open and more diverse," says Chelle. "The fifties ideal of the white American family with 2.2 kids doesn't cut it in today's world," Tina concludes.

Their Fund is the first of its kind in America. For Chelle and Tina, it is about "stopping the assumptions." On the street or at the grocery store, people stop to admire Grace and inevitably ask Chelle who the baby looks like, her or the father. Chelle tells them that Grace looks most like her *other* mom.

"It is not shocking or controversial—or unique anymore—to be really radical," smiles Tina. "Being radical today is what is perfectly ordinary. We can't think of anything that is more perfectly ordinary than raising children. We're lucky that Grace is a marvelous, wonderful, outgoing kid. I believe that it's because Chelle stays home with her. So, in some ways, we are the typical Ozzie and Harriet family."

"People ask, 'How do you do this? How do you raise a kid and not work?'" When asked these questions, Chelle replies, "'Well, my wife supports me.' They are completely amazed by that. It would never occur to Tina not to support me. We are family."

"Both of us had been in relationships before in which our partners didn't want to have kids," Tina says. "Both of us felt that it was important for our lives to have children—so talk about a match made in Heaven!"

They met in 1993 and were married in 1994.

"It just took off like a whirlwind," remembers Chelle.

By 1995, Tina was running for office, and Chelle was pregnant.

"We just—at the same kind of warp-speed—decided that, now that we were married, we should get started with the baby," laughs Tina. "The depth of our commitment to our relationship is shown in our taking on this responsibility together."

"I've never done anything quite so permanent before!" Chelle adds. "We've seen people who are the product of divorced households. It is hard on the kids. We don't want to do that to Grace. It is not an option. You can't leave, because it is your turn to put Grace to bed tonight!"

"Grace was three months old," Tina reminisces, "when I suddenly turned to Chelle and said, 'Oh my God! We are never going to be alone in this house again! She lives here!'"

Somehow, they manage to make time for each other, too, knowing that "we are going to have our relationship long after Grace hightails it to college and doesn't speak to us for five years—until she's thirty and realizes how smart we are!" Tina laughs.

THOUGH TINA AND CHELLE consider themselves "perfectly ordinary," they are aware that not everyone sees them that way. Their educational work is on-going—beginning with their commitment ceremony.

"We called it a wedding," explains Chelle. "We very intentionally used all the trappings and language of that tradition because that is what our families understood."

"Language is very precise," Tina continues. "When you use the term 'married' people understand what your relationship is to the other person. And they also, through generations of honoring those sorts of married relationships, understand that their role is to support the relationship. We are educating people in the gay and lesbian community about what it is like to have kids, too. Chelle works a lot harder during the day, chasing Grace, than I do. Even though I sometimes get yelled at by angry constituents, her boss is thirty-one inches tall and non-verbal!"

"There are not a lot of role models for lesbians who stay home, raising a child. So, I spend a lot of time with straight moms who realize that I am a mom just like them. I worry about the same things that they do. We talk about the same issues of child development. We talk about the same problems with our partners. It is the same thing."

"We've gotten to the point with some of these couples," Tina explains, "that they see no difference between a man and a woman or two women raising children. I think that we are a bridge to many different communities. Grace gets a real-life education in diversity. It will make her a citizen of the world."

Tina and Chelle are secure, financially and emotionally. They have a lot to offer their daughter. But as much as they give to Grace, she gives back to them.

"Raising Grace is a definite adventure. It is such a tremendous opportunity, such a gift, to be able to view the world through Grace's eyes. Missing from gay and lesbian relationships is a continuity of generations, feeling like you are passing something to the next generation—the learning, the care, the love—let them go forth and do good things in the world. We are both from blue-collar backgrounds. Chelle grew up on a farm, and, I'm the first generation kid of immigrants, the only one to go to college. My mom and dad worked in factories their whole lives. Now, here I am. I had an opportunity at Microsoft to make some money. I'm what America is supposed to be about. What I want to use my money for is to make the world a better place. To come out as an incredibly visible lesbian, I think, has changed the minds of a lot of people about who they can be. They didn't think two women could do this."

Melanie Hope & Catherine Gund

ELANIE HOPE AND CATHERINE GUND ARE
having a baby. They plan to have four or five children
together—depending on who you talk to.

Cat wants to be an integral part of Mel's pregnancy. She sleeps
with her back to Mel's stomach so they can both feel the baby kick.
She walks Mel to work every morning. She even has sympathy fatigue
and mood swings.

"It was really cute in the beginning when it was more comfortable
for Mel to wear dresses. I like her in dresses, but she didn't like them
'because people won't think I am a lesbian.' I realized that there is
this whole other thing—a pregnant lesbian! Mel doesn't want people
to think she is straight, which is something I don't ever deal with.
Nobody ever thinks I'm straight!"

"Now with me showing, it even confuses other lesbians," adds
Mel. "When I see them on the street, they don't know that I am a
dyke too. Also people are nicer to you when you are pregnant. In
some ways, I am safer."

On the subway people make room for the pregnant lady. Then,
noticing Cat, they slowly figure it out—and often slide over to make
space for her also.

Cat and Mel now see themselves differently, too. They are the only
lesbians in their birthing class, and the only couple in that environ-
ment, they feel, who truly treats the pregnancy as a cooperative effort.

"Not only will our kid have two parents, it will have two *mothers*,"
Mel explains. "That let Cat and I really imagine four kids with us
both still being able to pursue our own interests. We both get to work
and have a family—and everything. It's going to be *great*!"

CAT AND MEL ARE ABLE to choose most aspects of the life and
family that they are making together. Each child will have a different
donor father, and each will be of mixed race. They don't know the gender of this baby and joke that they will let the child decide for itself at
thirteen. Everything is up for discussion, including what it means to
be a couple.

"We started out being 'mistresses,'" laughs Cat. "I joke when I
say we are the married couple among our friends because they would
say that, but we never use that terminology. Mel and I have a really
trusting relationship, an open relationship. We are non-monogamous,
but we know where our commitment lies. We know that we are each
other's person forever. It works for both of us. It keeps us much more

involved in our community, in our own lives, and in better shape. It keeps us going out. In our case, it is not about actually having sex with other people, all the time. It is about really being comfortable with who you are, whether your girlfriend is there or not—and having that be part of what we love about each other."

MEL AND CAT LIVE by their own rules. "Certainly, in our situation, nothing comes automatically," explains Cat. "So, everything that happens is by our own choice. We work at it. Although in many situations heterosexual people don't have to consider their options and make choices and decisions, Mel and I had these very serious conversations about not only how we were going to raise our family but how we felt about children and what we would do if something happened to one of us. We have been deliberate. It was important to us not to replicate the nuclear family, a closed situation where there are a lot of secrets and boundaries between the family and society. We are all about everything just being open, known, and demystified. I think it makes people stronger to make their choices and decisions when they have as much information as possible."

"Our kids will have a lot of strengths to rely on," Mel continues. "We are really conscious of creating a home that gives them a lot of security and pride in who they are. They won't feel like, 'I have this problem, this thing I have to hide.' There is nothing at all to hide. You can get so caught up in being afraid."

"People keep saying to both of us, 'Oh, the baby is going to be biracial. You're in an interracial relationship. You're lesbians bringing up this kid. How's that gonna be?" says Cat. "All those things can be gifts! Everyone's got a story. A child growing up in any situation is going to have to deal. In this city and among our friends, there are kids with all different families. We've chosen to live in New York City because it is incredibly multi-racial and cross-class in totally blatant, scary, and contradictory ways that make it really comfortable for us to live here. It feels so normal to us.

"I grew up in a situation where the divorce was terrible. We want it to be really clear that this child does not come from a broken home. It comes from, if anything, a bigger-than-whole home. Mel's father says he can't imagine that lesbians shouldn't be supported in having children because all of the lesbians he's met are so extraordinary!"

Family and friends are so completely accepting of Cat and Mel having a baby that Cat's brother absentmindedly wondered if the baby would look like their side of the family, and another friend speculated that their baby might be big, since Cat is so tall.

As they have their family, Cat and Mel plan to take turns bearing the four or five children.

"I always thought, 'Oh, I'm butch, and I can't have a kid,'" remembers Cat. "I had so associated pregnancy with femininity. I realized that it is not about femininity in any other way than being a woman is about femininity. I am a woman. I've created being a woman in my own version. It's occurred to me that, yeah, I could do this. Being pregnant would be my version of being pregnant. I'd wear overalls and sweat pants. I don't have to look a certain way or act a certain way to be pregnant. And that's really exciting because it's freed me from all those constraints of what it means to be a girl and what it means to be feminine."

"I think a lot of women see pregnancy as this vulnerable thing in the same way that they buy into so many other things about what is feminine and what women should do," agrees Mel. "I don't feel like I am about to fall. And I haven't bought into the 'I need to shoot myself full of drugs so I don't feel anything because I can't give birth.' I think some women get talked into that. I feel totally fine. In fact, I feel more powerful having this belly. It is a really powerful, incredible feeling."

"I love that she is pregnant," says Cat. "I never knew pregnant women. I thought it was something that I would be scared of, excluded from, careful of. But being able to have a sexual relationship with someone who is pregnant is really intense. I think a lot of women don't let it be sexual or don't feel like it is sexy. People are like, 'You guys have been together so long and you're having sex and now Melanie's pregnant and you are still having sex!' They can't believe it."

As for the sexuality of their unborn children, Cat and Mel are happy for them to make their own choices. For themselves, they have discovered a new intimacy.

"I feel with Cat like she has to be here. I have to know where she is," says Melanie with some astonishment. "I am much more attached to her, literally. It is this amazing thing that is happening, and it is moving toward this even more amazing thing. We've gotten tighter in a way."

"We've really let this pregnancy be that kind of joint project," agrees Cat. "I mean, this isn't just Melanie. She's been really generous with me around the pregnancy. It really is *our* child. I can say that because I believe it. That has to come a lot from her, and it has. There is a real openness on both of our parts for what might come, and neither of us was like that before. Just the sense that we've committed to an unknown is a BIG commitment! Much bigger than saying 'OK, I can commit to buying a house with you.' In this case, we've said, 'I'm ready to do what needs to be done' and we don't even know what those things are! We are still very independent, but we are more stable both individually and together."

"Because there is this commitment it has taken the relationship to a different level." Melanie pauses, holding Cat's hand as she caresses her cheek. "If someone can totally love you through a pregnancy and be totally committed not only to you, but to this other person that is going to come out of you, it really is a big deal. To know that it is our baby, and that Cat is as excited about this baby as I am—you can't promise someone that. Even if there is a husband who is the biological father, you don't always get what I feel like I've gotten. In that sense, it is beyond loving me. I know this is real."

Deborah Cohen & Frances Ryan

"FRANCES RYAN, *I choose you to be my life partner. When I met you I was so swept up by attraction, it seemed like a fantasy—one that could never endure. In time, I began to recognize the ingredients for a journey of companionship nurtured by romance, affection, honesty, and humor. Our relationship embodies love's most profound possibilities. You are my B'sherta, my destiny. I love the woman you are, and the woman I am in your presence. I will love you, hold you, respect you, and cherish your uniqueness. I will stand up beside you and sleep in your arms. I choose you to hold me as your beloved in your heart, to be my heart's sanctuary and peace, and my body's closest friend. Nothing but your smile has made my heart so moved. Accept this ring, be my love, and we shall all the pleasures prove.*"

"DEBORAH COHEN, *from the moment we first met, I have been completely enchanted with you. Being with you has brought me more happiness and joy than I have ever known. The past four and a half years have been like a fairy-tale filled with romance, laughter, tenderness, and passion. Like a wild-flower, your love has swept across the landscape of my heart, clearing all that would smother the seeds of new beginnings. What has grown within me is the strength to be who I am and the courage to share myself with you wholly, openly, and honestly. I stand before you today—completely free of any doubts, free of any fears, free to give my heart to you, and free to share my life with you—my one and only love. Please accept this ring as a symbol of my pledge to you. Let it represent the wholeness and everlasting nature of my love. Let it remind you everyday that you are my beloved, and that I will forever hold you safely and tenderly in my heart.*"

THERE IS NO PLANNER for a Jewish-Irish-lesbian wedding. Arranging their perfect wedding day was a process that took Fran Ryan and Deb Cohen two years from proposal to ceremony.

"We felt like, if were gonna get married, we're gonna do it big. We're gonna do it with pride. Were gonna do it with chutzpa! Fran and I wanted people to look at us and say, 'Those women are so in love, and that's what it is all about.' We weren't getting hung up on all the rules. We were just so completely taken with each other."

For both women, their wedding day was the culmination of a

dream. Fran had long envisioned her bride. "I always had this image of this beautiful woman—big brown eyes, curly dark hair—and there she is! That is why I did not want to see Deborah before the ceremony. I came out and walked down the aisle—all nervous—and there's all these people looking at me. I stopped and turned around. I thought, 'This is it.' When the door opened, it was like a fantasy. It really was. But, it was happening, to me!"

"WHEN I WAS A LITTLE KID," remembers Deborah, "I never thought I was going to get married. I always thought that I was going to be alone my whole life. I didn't know why I thought that, but it made me very sad. Then as a teenager, when I was straight, I never thought I would get married because my average relationship lasted two weeks. I never liked anybody for too long. Then when I was older, I'd go to weddings and really feel like an outsider. I always thought, 'God, what it would be like to be one of those people! But it will never be me.' When Fran asked me to marry her, suddenly it's like, 'Wow, that could be me!' My friends all said that, too: 'We never thought this could be for us.' We should get to have all this stuff too. We need people to dance around us in circles. We need to celebrate our relationships. We need that. I just feel like my heart is so full now. I never thought that I would have this much love. I never thought I could receive it.

"One of the things that I thought about," Deb continues, "while we were planning all this was the discussion that was going on in Congress about how western civilization as we know it is going to crumble if gays and lesbians are allowed to marry each other. And

I thought, boy, you know, if straight people believe this, their relationships must not be very stable if they really think that my marrying Fran is going to pull the rug out from under their lives.

"When I was coming out, what impressed me about lesbians was that they were just making up their own rules as they went along and that was just so liberating. Everything about how women are supposed to be in the world is contrary to that. Women are not allowed to just make up their own lives as they go along. Women are not allowed to be the authors of their own existence; they are constantly having to please other people and sell themselves short.

"We've had some criticism from lesbians about us getting married, and I can understand that because in the beginning I thought, 'Oh this is patriarchal and sexist.' But when two women marry it just doesn't mean that. It can't mean that.

"Our marriage forces people to reconsider what it means for two people to come together. We created our own ceremony. We made our own promises. You can create your own relationship—your own life. This isn't about one of us owning the other. This is just about the two of us being together and loving each other. In the lesbian community there is a lot of flirting that goes on with people who are involved. I think that it isn't supportive of our relationship. This is our way of saying Fran and I are not available. We are with each other. If somebody starts flirting with me I won't be flattered by it. I will feel that they are not respecting my life choice and my relationship.

"Not every woman should get married, this should not be everybody's choice, but for the women who want to do it, it should be respected."

A T THE RECEPTION HELD IN a country inn near Northampton, Fran's father sang and Deborah's father toasted his new daughter-in-law. The newlyweds were showered with good wishes.

"My mother keeps coming up to me and singing, 'Sadie, Sadie, Married Lady!'" laughs Deborah. "For us to make it, we need the support and wisdom—and love—of our families. We need people to know that they are not there just as an audience. They're making a commitment to us. They are going to nurture our relationship."

"People have asked me, 'Why are you going to do it, because it is not going to be legal anyway?'" Fran recalls. "But the ceremony and the ritual isn't what legalizes heterosexual relationships. The piece of paper is what legalizes it—and that is the only thing that Deborah and I don't have. Frankly, I wouldn't mind having it, but it certainly isn't going to legitimize my relationship anymore. I say to her in private, 'I love you and will always be there for you.' That has meaning and weight to it. But now, we have said it in the presence of our family and friends, and that has a different weight to it."

"Fran never misses an opportunity to tell me that she thinks I'm beautiful or that she loves me," smiles Deborah. "When I came down the aisle, Fran gasped. Sometimes when I come home from work, she looks at me that same way—like it is the first time. She never stops falling in love with me, and I never stop falling in love with her."

"Do you know, the wait staff came up to us after our reception and told us that they have done hundreds of weddings but that this is the best wedding they have ever done," Fran says proudly.

"The bartender said that our waltz moved him to tears!" adds Deb.

Patricia Field & Rebecca Weinberg

"We have two different versions of our meeting, my version and Pat's version. Hers is the most accurate. I tend to exaggerate a little bit."

According to Pat Field, they met in a club where the twenty-year-old Rebecca Weinberg was go-go dancing. Pat, an established forty-seven-year-old designer whose self-named clothing store is a well-known Greenwich Village landmark, caught Rebecca's eye as she walked past her cage. Rebecca leaned down and said, "Hi, my name is Yo-Yo. I'd like to take you out to dinner sometime."

"My immediate reaction was that I liked her straight-forwardness, so I said 'Sure, why not?' and that's the way it started."

"People say that I knew who she was," remembers Rebecca, "but I really didn't. I was naïve, and that's a good thing. I just saw this woman. She caught my eye. She sparkled. I went for it. I was attracted to her charisma. She just had this incredible aura around her. She's a star, and I'm a star. We can both carry a room—trust me."

"I always took it as one day at a time because we were at such different stages in our lives," Pat reminisces. "I just tried to stay on that realistic beat. When we first started going together, there was a huge buzz around us. I guess it was a little bit shocking." Their twenty-seven-year age difference distressed friends who warned Pat she was headed for trouble. Rebecca's friends couldn't understand the attraction.

"We ignored them totally because we were so caught up. Pat and I had a lot of fire, intense passion, and it's lasted."

Pat and Rebecca don't dismiss their age difference, they value it.

"Pat has more energy, more get-up-and-go than I ever had," laughs Rebecca. "She's lived more life than me. I'm like a student of sorts. I compare everybody to Pat. Pat's a nut. I love her uniqueness. She marches to her own drummer, and so do I. I was extremely attracted to Pat's joie de vive. I wanted to experience finer things, and she was totally willing to teach me. She was worldly and educated. I found that very attractive. I was always attracted to older women."

"Rebecca teaches me as well," Pat adds. "She keeps me up to date. I live in a young world. I don't find anyone else out there who attracts me. No one compares to what Rebecca is to me. Rebecca is a gorgeous, vivacious woman. Women are lined up to be with her. That's a reality for me. If I got neurotic over it, I would be miserable."

REBECCA AND PAT DIVIDE THEIR TIME between a four-story walk-up above Pat's store in Greenwich Village and their home in Miami.

"It's fun!" exclaims Rebecca. "When I wake up in the morning, I am the happy girl — a bouncing baby girl. There is nothing very routine about our life. I have fun with Pat. She keeps me entertained. She keeps surprising me. She works at our relationship without acknowledging she's working at it."

Their life together is only conventional in one aspect: Rebecca has worked very hard to make their house a home, for both of them.

"When Rebecca moved in here she filled it with herself, which made it more complete. I am finding myself being happier at home than I have ever been in my life."

"I wanted to be taken care of for a while," Rebecca explains. "When I met Pat I really sort of rooted myself for the first time. It was an opportunity to make a life. Because I never had that as a child, I wanted to dig my roots deep, and I have."

Rebecca first ran away at thirteen and has been on her own since she was fifteen. She hung out with bands, worked as a housegirl for two gay women who were dancers and prostitutes, and also worked briefly in the adult entertainment world. "My history is full of twists and turns. I was very adventurous," she declares.

Together, Pat and Rebecca do costume designing and styling for TV and film. Rebecca, who "does a little bit of everything," also models

Pat's line, but is best known as a cabaret performer and a Drag King.

"I'm a real Sibyl of characters," Rebecca laughs. With success comes the sense that Rebecca is just now making a life for herself.

"I make it with Pat, but I am becoming more independent."

"It's your life," Pat encourages, "you've got to live it. You can't look back and say, 'I've put myself in someone else's life and not had my own.'"

PAT AND REBECCA ARE FREE SPIRITS who share a libertarian belief in the transformative power of free enterprise, see marriage as a "legal entanglement," and most of all don't want to "jump on any bandwagon. I do not operate as a gay person, I operate as a person. What I want in my life is independence," Pat declares. "I want to be free. I don't want anybody telling me what to do."

The value that they place on freedom influences their sense of commitment. They believe they will always have a relationship — whether of love or friendship. "If we enjoy being together, we're together," is how Rebecca sees it. "When I met Pat, I thought that she was fascinating. If it takes me a whole lifetime to know her, great."

Pat shares her pragmatic view. "I don't have control over the future, so how can I dare to say, 'We are going to be together for life and that is it?' I would love it, but I can't legislate it. Everyone's life is their own and that is all, really, that they have. The way I feel about Rebecca, they way she makes me happy, the way we have our life together — of course, I want it to go on. But if it can't, I will always love Rebecca for that beautiful time that we spent together."

Antoinette Pregil & Tammy Rodrigues

"**O**NE DAY, ABOUT EIGHT YEARS AGO, I WAS reading the Sunday paper," Tammy Rodrigues recalls, "and at the bottom of the front page, it said, 'If you're gay and you want to get married, contact Bill Woods.' So I thought we could get married legally! I thought he was going to take us to get a license and just get married. But it didn't happen that way. When we went down there, we didn't know that the news people were going to be there. There were two other couples there, too. They turned all of us down. Bill Woods said that we were going to have a case because the license didn't specify male and female, but still the state said that we couldn't get married. I was disappointed. Big time. We went to the ACLU; they wouldn't touch it. That's when Bill Woods said, 'We'll go talk to this lawyer, Dan Foley. He's very open-minded.' When we went to see Dan and explained everything, he agreed to take the case."

Their case was thrown out the first time, but Antoinette Pregil and Tammy Rodrigues appealed. On May 5, 1993, the Supreme Court of Hawaii ruled that the state must provide a "compelling" reason to justify its discrimination against same-sex couples. When the state was unable to do so, the court ruled in the couple's favor. The ruling is now being appealed, but Toni and Tammy hope that it will be upheld.

"There is so much *Aloha* in Hawaii," says Toni of the state that is known for its tolerance: It was the first to legalize abortion, the first to ratify the ERA, and probably will be the first to legalize gay marriage.

"*Aloha* means love, *Aloha* means hello, *Aloha* means everything. So I feel like if it is going to change, Hawaii is going to change it."

"Just a little dot on the globe . . ." muses Tammy.

". . . in a whole ocean of love," finishes Toni.

TONI AND TAMMY BOTH WERE BORN and raised on Oahu, where they now live.

"We met at a high school dance," smiles Toni. "I was eighteen. She was only fifteen. About a week later, I saw her walking with a surf board and found out she had left home. I just said, 'Come and stay with me.' We were together for five years. We lived as a couple on our own, until she started to stray. I guess she was a little bit too young. We ended up breaking up."

One day, ten years later, when Toni ran into Tammy's mother, she asked her to pass on her phone number and say hello.

"I came home from work and Tammy had called. We ended up

taking a drive. We drove around for hours just talking, catching up on all the years. We talked about our ex-girlfriends. I told her all about my daughter. I dropped her off and as soon as I got home, the phone rang. It was her. She just wanted to make sure that I got home alright. She asked me out for the following Saturday."

"She was my first true love," smiles Tammy. "You always think about your first, even if you're apart. She was perfect. I wanted her to be the one that would last for the rest of my life. As you get older, you realize that you made mistakes. I always wondered, 'Why did I screw up?' It was the best thing that I ever had—and I screwed it up. I never thought we would ever be back together again. You just hope you'll meet somebody else like that, and not make the same mistake again.

"The second time around it was more solid," explains Tammy. "I grew up. This time I knew that I wanted to marry her. I knew that this was it. I lost it once. I don't want it to happen again. When you get married and have problems, you work them out. You don't just divorce. I'm only going to get married once and that's it. It will never happen again for me."

"Marriage is sacred," agrees Toni. "I believe in God. In the Bible, it says that living with someone and not being married is a sin. Once we get married, we will be under God's wing. That's just the way I feel. A commitment ceremony is not for real—and we are real people. I also can't see how these heterosexual couples can get married today and divorced next week. It's not supposed to be that way. I guess because it is so easy for them. If they were put through what we are going through now, they'd think twice about it."

TONI LOST HER FAMILY over the issue of gay marriage. "When my father saw the news, he totally flipped. He was on the war path. I cannot repeat what he said to me. I am the oldest. Everybody depended on me for moral support, financial support, babysitting, a place to stay, and all that kind of good stuff. We spent weekends together, barbecued. And then all of a sudden, because we want to get married and be happy, it is like, 'Oh, no, no! Why did you have to tell the world? Why isn't it enough for you to live as you are living now?' Well, I can tell you why—I want the same things they have."

TAMMY AND TONI HAVE NEVER considered withdrawing from the case that they are pursuing with two other gay couples, but, until recently, they avoided being in the public eye.

"Everybody asked, 'Three couples? There's only *two* couples!' That's how in the background we were," Tammy remembers. "At the beginning, we really didn't think it was going to turn out this way. We didn't want to put our daughter through something like that. So we just backed off and let it mellow out a bit."

"We thought that if the family acted the way they did, other people would too," remembers Toni. "And you know what? It was just the family. Other people, they were great!"

Finally, it was their daughter Lena, now twenty-one years old, who encouraged them to step into the fray.

"Dan called us to let us know there was going to be an important hearing," Tammy explains. "He wanted us to be there. And when Lena found out about it, she said, 'You have to do it. You came this far. You have to fight for your happiness—really fight for what we believe in.' So we did."

THEY HAVE NOW BEEN QUOTED, questioned, interviewed, photographed, and filmed countless times. They even appeared on *Rolanda*.

"We were scared. At the very first TV interview I could barely talk. I could barely answer questions," Toni recalls. "I don't feel like we are famous or anything. But I think, 'Wow, I just can't believe this will go down in history.'"

"I don't think about it like that," counters Tammy. "I never thought it would go on this long and I never thought it would be this big. If it's not a big deal at work with the guys or at home with my neighbors, then why is it a big deal for everybody else? I just wish it would come to an end soon. It's taking up too much time, too much of the state's money. Why doesn't the state just butt out and use the money for other things? If they're so worried about children why don't they use the money for children who are being abused? We are taxpayers. We are not harming anybody, we are just minding our own business. We should be able to do the exact same thing as everybody else. There's so many things we can't do unless we can get married. When our daughter was young, I could have given her health benefits. She could have been eligible for scholarships through my job. It's a whole bunch of stuff that a lot of people don't even think about."

"There is too much prejudice in this world," continues Toni. "People don't know who we really are, so how can they condemn us?

If we can accomplish getting gay marriage legalized, maybe we can make people see that we are like everybody else. To me, getting married will mean finally being accepted. We have something to look forward to now. Otherwise, our relationship comes to a standstill. It shouldn't be that way. I don't know what the difference is between a heterosexual couple and a gay couple—I clean house, she cleans the yard. The only difference is the sex. And we're not asking you to sleep with us! I think people have these attitudes because they are afraid they might get sucked in and become gay themselves."

"And," adds Tammy, "if they feel like that they probably have some gayness in them!"

THE MOST RECENT RULING CAME on December 3, 1996—their anniversary. "Our daughter Lena called me at work," Toni says. "She was crying, she was so happy. She had champagne ready and everything." But they still have to wait through the appeal process.

"If I was told I could get married right now, I wouldn't really want a big wedding," says Tammy. "I just want that paper that says that we are legally married and that nobody can take it away from us. I say that's 'our daughter,' but then she will *really be* my daughter, and my son-in-law will *legally be* my son-in-law, and our grandson—I will really be his grandma. It would mean so much. What it'll mean is that we'll finally be able to get married—and live and die as one. I will have married the person that I loved."

"I want to know," Toni declares, "that, when I die, we will be together. She will always be there in my heart. It is forever. Eternity. That is what it means to me."

Kelli Peterson & Erin Wiser

KELLI PETERSON AND ERIN WISER HAD ALREADY been dating a year when they attended a lecture by Candace Gingrich.

"I was excited about going," remembers Kelli, "but I didn't think as many people were going to be there as showed up. I remember the way Candace was talking about getting involved and coming out in your community. It was inspiring—the general feeling of her speech. I felt there was something I could do."

"Candace said nobody should wait to be an activist," continues Erin. "We had already been thinking about clubs for a long time, but that really solidified it."

Shortly after attending that talk, Kelli and Erin founded the Gay/Straight Alliance as an extra-curricular school club. The club's aim was to let gay youth know that there were others out there like them and to include straight kids who were supportive. They knew from experience how isolating being gay could be. At the time, Kelli was a senior and Erin a junior at East High School in Salt Lake City, Utah. Kelli and Erin didn't see any reason why the Gay/Straight Alliance shouldn't be just another extra-curricular school club. Twenty-five other students agreed.

In response to the Gay/Straight Alliance, the local school board banned all extra-curricular clubs. The Utah state legislature enacted a state-wide injunction against school organizations dealing with "human sexuality." Two years later, Kelli and Erin's club still makes headlines in Salt Lake City. Barred from meeting during school time, they now rent a classroom after hours, as all taxpayers are entitled to do. Kelli was the first president, and after she graduated, Erin took over. They are still petitioning to become a bona fide school club, but their present goal is "just existing," and so far they have succeeded.

The club—more accurately, Kelli and Erin themselves—has made a real difference. During Kelli's freshman year, there was only one out student. Kelli was repeatedly beaten up by a gang of five girls in her gym class. When she complained to her gym teacher, she was essentially told, "That's what you get for being different." But by the time Kelli graduated, she and Erin attended a Gay Prom organized by other gay classmates. There will be two hundred students attending Erin's Gay Prom.

"There are so many more cliques now than the losers and the winners," says Erin. "I like high school a lot more for not having to bend over my paper and clutch my pen when someone is making a queer

joke. I can turn around and tell my favorite queer joke—making a total ass of them—because everyone but this person knows that I am gay. I have a lot more fun."

Now, two of Salt Lake City's four high schools have gay and lesbian clubs. Though Kelli and Erin feel the "whole state is generally hostile," they have no plans to leave. Being activists in Salt Lake City is an opportunity to give something back to the gay and lesbian community that supports them.

"There is so much to do!" exclaims Kelli.

Kelli and Erin are aware of how much has already been accomplished, and how different their era is from that of their lesbian predecessors.

"It is almost impossible to be in high school and not be sexual, period," Erin describes. "Whereas in generations past everything was puppy love and such—you see that now in the third grade. It is hard to find a sixteen-year-old virgin. We'd look weirder not doing anything than being lesbians."

O N SCHOOL NIGHTS, Kelli and Erin used to talk on the phone from 10 P.M. till 4 A.M. and then go to school after only two hours of sleep. During one summer when Erin was grounded and banned from the phone for three months, they sent letters and notes and snuck phone calls from work. "We've survived things that usually break teenage relationships," notes Erin with pride. "I took saying, 'I love you' very seriously, so did Kelli. She was on the phone with me one night when she said, 'I think I am falling in love with you.' Right then—the dam broke—all these

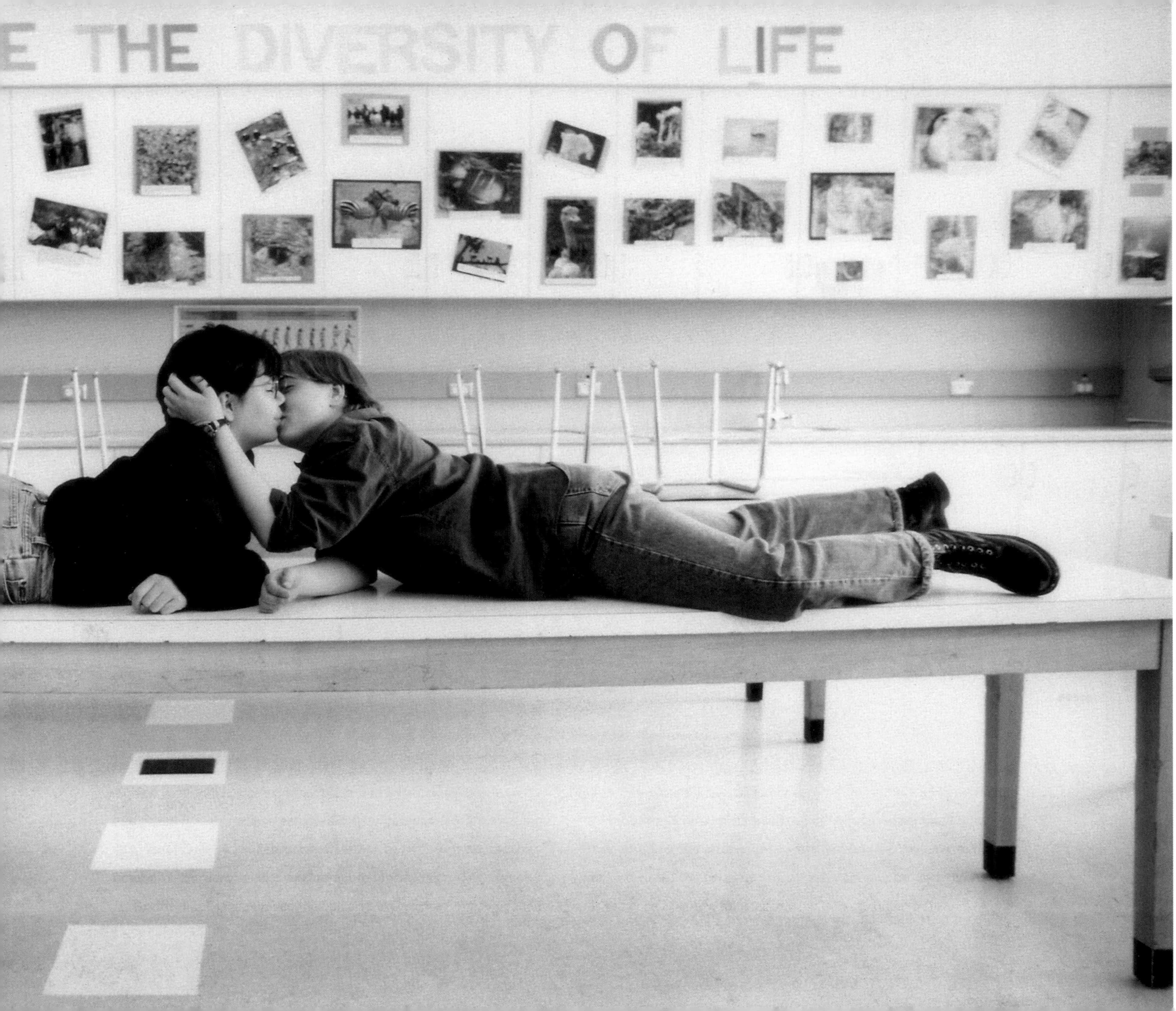
E THE DIVERSITY OF LIFE

emotions that I had just really been pushing back were right there in front of me. It was okay to admit to them. I had really fallen in love with Kelli."

"It was never just dating. Once Erin and I were together, we were always together."

"When I knew what love meant, what fighting for it meant, because I had to suffer for it, it gave me direction. It gave me meaning. It gave me a lot."

Erin realized that she was a lesbian around the age of thirteen, "with much thanks to the *Rocky Horror Picture Show*. I was attracted to Tim Curry in drag. I was up all night thinking about that. Eventually, it dawned on me that it was because he looked very feminine. Then, I went to a Mormon girls camp and hid in my sleeping bag for a week. I thought about it some more. I think it dawned on my parents when I was about three years old—I told them that God had made a mistake in making me a girl."

Erin grew up in a Mormon family and describes herself as a "Jack Mormon," a lapsed Mormon, rather than as a "Molly Mormon," the more devout variety. She has now left the faith entirely due to her impression of the Mormon church's stand on homosexuality.

"Murder is forgivable, homosexuality is curable. Good Mormons don't use lesbian, gay, or homosexual as nouns, because that implies that this is a form of identification, a person, as opposed to a choice and a practice."

Kelli's own Mormon upbringing made coming out more difficult for her. "When I realized that I was gay, I didn't want to be gay. Everything that I'd seen or heard about gay people from the Mormon Church was that they were sick and disgusting. They all had AIDS and were going to die. I decided that it was just not going to be me. I set about trying to cover it up."

As a result of her self-repression, Kelli was chronically depressed. She was eventually hospitalized, diagnosed with Gender Identity Disorder, and treated with "reparative therapy."

"Their idea of treatment is forcing you to wear very girlie clothes, make-up, and do your hair. They wouldn't allow me to touch anybody of the same sex, or even look at them. I think it's a crock. It could have made me much weaker in many ways, but it made me stronger. I turned into a rather demanding person when I was fifteen or sixteen years old. I started demanding that my parents respect me for who I am and who I'm becoming. Nobody should ever have to go through any of that. That is what the Gay/Straight Alliance is all about. I've been through quite a lot and have come to the point·of being okay with myself and with being out."

They credit feminism for freeing them to redefine what it means to be a woman.

"I don't think that I could live in any other time," Erin asserts. "Women are presented with so many choices today. I have the freedom not to have a feminine identity, the freedom to just be as androgynous as I'd like to be. Just the fact that a third grader knows what a faggot is—I mean as negative as that sounds—it's helped us."

"Now there is so much more information," agrees Kelli. "TV, Internet, magazines, books, even television shows have gay characters, which is something you would never have seen before. I think that it is a very big cultural and social change that has led us to being where we are now. In Utah, a woman's life is predestined for her. But my life wasn't written for me when I began admitting to being a lesbian. Being a lesbian means being in a truly equal relationship."

"My parents always said I could be whatever I wanted," adds Erin. "I took that liberty."

The perseverance they have already shown is proof they aren't afraid of growing up together.

"I can see us changing a lot," Erin says. "And, when we do change, we tend to fall in love all over again. We realize that we've become different people—and that is just as cool as it was before."

Kelli and Erin have just recently gotten an apartment together. Kelli works two jobs while Erin finishes school. Their parents compete to see who can be more supportive. For Christmas, Kelli got so much Gay Pride paraphernalia that they are thinking of redecorating the apartment in rainbows.

Eventually, they plan to go to college together. Kelli wants to study nursing, while Erin hopes to study sociology as she is particularly interested in religious culture. Erin isn't sure if she still subscribes to the Mormon belief that marriage is for all time and eternity, "but I have a feeling that we'll always be connected. I love how Kelli makes me feel. Although I have always been really, really unemotional, she is able to make me admit that I'm angry, that I am hurt. She can make me cry. She's so passionate! She deals with things. She goes out and changes things. She's an ass-kicker. And she's got this real feminine side that she hides behind a short haircut and a leather jacket—like she wears a nightie. It's so funny!"

"I'm gonna kick your ass right now!" laughs Kelli. "Butch and femme is a running joke with us. People consider me the female in our relationship and right now I work full time at one job and part time at the other to pay the rent and buy the food and keep her fed and clothed and in school. I'm the breadwinner, but I'm also 'the female.' I find that funny. I always found Erin to be very boyish and very cute—that's what attracted me to her. I love that she is so calm. She's able to look at things from a more balanced point of view. And, I love that she has *no* feminine side!"

"Hey, I wear a bra!" Erin shouts with a laugh.

Sally Boyle & Erin Shoemaker

"SOME PEOPLE SAY, 'IT IS NOT POSSIBLE TO READ the Bible as approving of homosexuality,'" begins Erin Shoemaker, an ordained minister in the United Church of Canada. "I would respond that it's not possible to read the Bible as supporting discrimination against anyone. Jesus came to cast a fire on the earth, and I am almost certain that he expects us all to be part of the kindling."

"Well, I wouldn't mind being the kindling if people would stop throwing water on the spark!" laughs Sally Boyle—also an ordained minister. "I've always known I was a shit-disturber, and I say that with a certain amount of pride at this point. Erin and I are a couple who passionately seek justice. I had long been attracted to Erin's peacefulness, her spirituality. I felt like my life was very chaotic, and Erin was the calm at the center of the storm. Her gentleness, her absolute commitment, and her tenacity are all qualities that I wrap up in the word love. Erin saw me as I truly am. Indeed, I saw her as she truly is. So now, instead of being the passionate pulpit-beater on my own, those things, we bring together to offer. There is something beyond us that is extremely important to us."

"ERIN AND I HAVE CERTAINLY had our relationship tested. We've been to the wall on it. In a town this size, we cannot hide."

Living and working in a small rural community, Sally and Erin have faced prejudice head-on.

"I think most people don't have any sense of what they ask us to do," continues Sally. "We often won't embrace one another in our own home without the curtains drawn. In Matthew, Jesus talks about dancing at one another's weddings and weeping at one another's funerals. That never happens for us. People don't dance at our weddings, and they don't weep at our grievings."

"It makes me sad that we used to walk along holding hands, and I realize that we haven't done that in the two years since we came here," adds Erin. "But I am most aware, when everything is really tough outside, that the one thing we have is the strength of our relationship. We survive things together. Our passion for justice is much more important. And people are already saying, 'We're different because you've been here.' That's wonderful."

"We've come a long way in twelve years," says Sally. "We're not there yet, but we've come a long way."

Susan Johnson & Connie Wolfe

"To Connie, who was the reason for it all," reads the dedication to Susan Johnson's book, *Staying Power: Long Term Lesbian Couples.* Susan was in love with "this perfectly wonderful woman," and determined to make it last. She had had a series of failed relationships, so she began her nationwide study of one hundred and eight lesbian couples. "I thought, well, I've got to find out how to do this, because I'm obviously not good at it! I should go talk to the experts. I picked ten years as the official definition of long-term because that meant somebody who had stayed in a relationship longer than I had!"

What Susan learned surprised her. The first lesson was about hanging in there when things get tough. "Not just mildly unhappy, but it could get miserable," Susan explains. She was amazed at the really difficult issues that couples could get beyond. They didn't necessarily solve them, but they could see past them to still stay together. Susan had always operated on the opposite principle.

"If things weren't happy all the time, then it meant that there was something the matter with the relationship, so you should leave to find one that was going to be happy all the time."

Of all the couples that Susan interviewed, there wasn't a single one that agreed with her on that point. "They just thought that was laughable," Susan says. "It was the most hysterical idea that they ever heard in their lives. It was very sobering for me. In fact, I hated finding that out."

Although she didn't like what she was hearing, Susan had a sense these women were talking about the real thing. "Romance was about getting together, and reality was about staying together."

Susan Johnson and Connie Wolfe have certainly experienced romance. When their relationship began, it was overwhelming, unexpected, and infused with a sense of destiny.

"It is like having been on a search that I didn't quite know I was on," remembers Connie. "I almost feel like the spirits in the universe picked me out, put me down in front of Susan, and said, 'Okay, here you go. You get to do it this lifetime.' It was just a miracle. This wasn't like any other falling-in-love I had ever done before. It was much more visceral—both carnal and spiritual at the same time."

Susan and Connie had a private commitment ceremony at their home in Anchorage in 1987.

For Connie and Susan, staying together offers the greatest possibility. "You think that you're changing when you are changing partners, but, in fact, you're just doing the same pattern over and over again," explains Susan. "All you do is keep meeting yourself in a different setting, and you never learn anything past that."

"As each year goes by, we're charting new emotional territory. It's been wonderful for me to keep pushing past my limits," says Connie. "Once I got past that watershed, all of a sudden I felt like I had a life."

Among the joys of being a long-term couple, says Susan, is their sense of progress. "One of the tragedies of breaking up is that you loose huge chunks of your own history, because you shared that history with whoever that person was, and when they're gone, that past is gone. If you stay with somebody you don't lose your own past. You can feel yourselves day by day building this history that is, God willing, going to continue." Connie is the archivist of the relationship. She has compiled photo albums commemorating each year of their relationship, since 1984. "You get to go through *life* together. It is just more fun. Each day becomes more dear to you. It is a richness of all those years and all that time."

SUSAN DESCRIBES HERSELF as a "born lesbian"—she has always felt this way. Connie, however, is a "born-again lesbian." She was married twice, had a son, and at the age of thirty-two fell in love with a woman. "I was very successful as a heterosexual. It was a shock for me actually to find that I could have feelings for women. Once I named it, I thought, 'Fabulous, I have just broken this terrible barrier. Now, I can really have a choice about what I do and who I love.' It was like the whole world opened up. God blessed me." Connie knows that she was not a "secret lesbian"

all those years: "It is absurd to think gay is genetic as far as women are concerned. Many women can in fact come to a cross-roads and choose."

"Which of course is a very threatening idea," adds Susan. "That means any woman can be a lesbian."

CONNIE AND SUSAN ARE VERY CLEAR about the advantages of loving women. "From the time I was little I have wanted to be known," says Connie. "Between men and women in this culture, it is impossible to be known. You certainly are able to be appreciated, to be loved, to be respected, but not known. In a lesbian relationship there were no differences to hide behind." As a lesbian, Connie found "something that fits more for your soul than for your role. I got thrown back into myself. I could know the person I really was, because I couldn't take 'the female role.' Ultimately I was choosing the road toward equality. Also, 'born lesbians' have a sense of female sexuality which begins outside a gender role. I get to be the subject of my sexuality as opposed to the object of it." And, most important, Connie discovered and received a different love: "I kept thinking, this is the kind of love I've been giving and now I am getting it back. This is why everyone loves women; this is why women love women and this is why men love women. It was wonderful."

For Connie and Susan this is the heart of the matter: "Lesbianism is so shocking," says Susan, "because lesbians actually *love* women. Lesbians always complain about not having role models when in fact we *are* role models."

While the born lesbian has often spent a lifetime internalizing homophobia, the born-again lesbian is proud: "You cannot shame me about being a lesbian," proclaims Connie. "I chose to be a lesbian. I love being a lesbian. I know the difference. You can't get me to not trust my own experience on this one. I felt fine as a heterosexual and I feel fine as a lesbian."

Now Connie and Susan have passed the ten-year mark themselves, and they have learned some things along the way. They don't say hurtful things. They never argue in the bedroom. They do invite friends to intervene when problems arise: "The presence of somebody else defuses the issue. You can't get as weird. The whole culture contains heterosexual relationships, they want them to work, they support them. We have to be more intentional."

If you ask, Connie will say this is the easiest relationship she has ever been in. Susan, on the other hand, will call it the most difficult. They used to argue over who was right until they had a "surreal" insight: "Even though we are two people sharing a life, we are not in the same relationship at all!" laughs Susan. "I live inside myself and my context is Connie. That is a *totally* different experience than Connie, who is inside herself, and her context is me. I don't even know what I look like to her! It is very weird." In Susan and Connie's expert opinion the best advice is to "really love the relationship that you are having," says Susan. "My God, can you imagine starting over!? We know each other's quirks, have gotten past being annoyed by them. We have a sense of humor about it. Connie is the best thing that ever happened to me."

Amanda Bearse & Dell Pearce

AMANDA BEARSE WAS ONE OF THE FIRST Hollywood actresses to come out—long before Ellen Degeneres or k.d. lang. For eleven seasons Amanda Bearse played the heterosexual Marcy D'Arcy on *Married with Children*. She has been that rare commodity, an openly gay actress in Hollywood.

"For years, I was the only out lesbian series regular in the television industry. I could've come out and they'd cancel the show, not because I was gay, but because it's in its eleventh year! Hollywood is dictated by money, as most big business is. The huge incomes that are attainable force you to make choices that don't necessarily serve your soul—not just about whether to come out of the closet. I think Hollywood is comfortable limiting actors anyway. You don't know what the public is going to like. That is why it is not a science, it is a risk. Here I am, I've got two strikes against me: I have been so exposed as one character for so long, and people also have a perception of my personal life. Oh, and I'm aging, too! So, it's a good thing I direct now!"

Amanda lives with her partner, Dell Pearce, and their daughters. Recently, they found themselves under increasing public scrutiny during a contentious custody battle with Dell's former partner, also a woman.

"There is a heightened sense of accountability that our community places on out celebrities," notes Dell. "A responsibility to live your life in a certain way to reflect what their expectations are. You have to stay grounded about who you are really responsible to and for—not doing something because it is what somebody else expects but being true to yourself. There is a lot of expectation . . ."

". . . and not a lot of us," finishes Amanda, "so the focus can be turned up pretty hot at times, because unfortunately we're spread so thin."

AMANDA AND DELL are more concerned with their family than the big business of Hollywood. Dell works from home, ensuring that someone is always there for their daughters. They have moved to a safer, suburban neighborhood where the girls can ride their bikes and go to public schools.

"It is more important to us to be out lesbians for our children," says Amanda of the publicity surrounding gay celebrities. "What we need to do is present positive, honest examples for our children in the world. At pre-school, they don't really care what I do for a living—just that I show up to do the room-mother duties."

WHEN DELL AND AMANDA MET, they were both raising young daughters and commiserated about the struggle to balance motherhood and work. They had another bond, too.

"Here in L.A.," Amanda explains, "we're both displaced southern women. Southern people find a sense of home in one other. Your heart is always there, so it's nice to find a piece of it miles and miles away."

Dell and Amanda were married by an Episcopal priest in Nashville, on New Year's Eve 1994. "It was important to us, for our children, to have that. We are very traditional people, in a very untraditional kind of way!" says Amanda.

"For me, it means Amanda and I are building a family," says Dell. "It is not just about committing to each other. We already had families, so we married them to each other, too."

"When you have children you don't fall in love alone," adds Amanda. "We feel very strongly that we chose each other, so we have to be a united, strong base for our children. This is where it began; this is why we are all four together. We are very instinctive mothers, Dell and me. Neither of us tries to parent the other's children. There's a time to take a front seat and a back seat."

"Amanda and I integrate our families as we go along, because there are certainly no rules to go by."

"Blended families are hard anyway, whether you have the license or the legal right to do it. When you take children along on your journey and ask them to make this adjustment, you are asking a great deal. It's not without bumpy roads. We are four very intense women in this family. We live life very strongly, and there are lots of emotions flying around all the time. Some need to be reigned in a little bit, but

we live life fully. We enjoy sharing that with each other. We have a lot of fun. The joy is just incredible. We say the word 'work' a lot, but it has an enormous payoff."

Dell and Amanda are clear about what they want and are not prepared to compromise.

"I would rather not be with anyone than be in a relationship where my needs weren't met," declares Dell.

Amanda considers their future with southern practicality. "We're not just messing around here. We do mean business. This is not something frivolous. To grow old together, that would be really a triumph. To be able to hold each other's hands while we watch our children grow—it's a forever commitment. The expectation is pretty high and the commitment strong."

The payoff for Dell and Amanda is having the kind of relationship they've always wanted. Both had "complicated histories" that they didn't want to repeat.

"I was thirty-five years old, with a child, with enough life experience behind me, that I knew what my needs were. I knew myself well enough to know Amanda was a person I could enjoy growing old with—that I could parent with. I could take on her rituals and traditions as my own and share mine with her. You get to a place where you know what you want, and I think we were both at that place. We knew that we could do this together. I love Amanda's spirit. There is enormous intensity, but there is a lightness, too. She's beautiful, very funny, and playful. She helps me embrace the child in myself."

". . . and I like the grown-up in Dell!" laughs Amanda. "One of the things that I love the most about Dell is that she's a real grown-up.

Being in the entertainment industry, there is this quest for perpetual youth—real juvenile behavior, attitudes—and I have a really low tolerance for it, especially in things that I value, like raising children."

"The celebrity aspect of who Amanda is is not why I fell in love with her," adds Dell. "The dichotomy of who she is and what she plays is so vast. Marcy doesn't live here—Amanda does!"

"Dell had never even seen my show!" continues Amanda. "This is a relationship of equality regardless of where the spotlight is shining. We know in our hearts where we are with one another, and that is what matters most to me. There is not much I feel I could do now without her. It is so nice to have someone who you love and trust to unburden with—and to help you carry the load and enjoy life, too, to go out and play."

MAKING TIME FOR FUN is something they take seriously. They appreciate the small rather than grand gestures—the notes Dell puts in Amanda's lunch box, pulling the kids in the wagon, singing around the piano, walks and talks.

"You have to find time for romance, though, with ready-made families," says Amanda. "Dell and I are very romantic and emotional. Our relationship is very passionate. It is important to us. It has to stay that way because it is real easy to put each other on down the list. We need our time alone and get real cranky if we don't get it. It's important to have that intimacy in bed and out of bed. It carries you through, it sustains you. It's why we are in this situation—because we fell in love with each other."

Lisa Kung & Iris Sandkühler

WHEN LISA KUNG AND IRIS SANDKÜHLER MET they were "smitten," but it seemed like such bad timing. Iris, who had just had a painful breakup, didn't wanted to get serious yet, and it was Lisa's last summer in Georgia. She was moving to New York in three months to start law school. Nothing about their circumstances seemed right, except each other.

"My personality can be overbearing, and you don't want a partner who gets threatened by that," says Lisa. "Iris has a very strong personality in a whole different way. If you can find two people with strong characters and it complements instead of clashing—that's so unusual—I think that's what we've got."

"If you are self-confident," agrees Iris, "you start to attract a lot of people that might not be. On a good day, they get some of that from you. On a bad day, they drag you down. With Lisa, I don't have to compromise or placate somebody's ego. It works for me because there is no struggle here."

Both are equally independent and ambitious. Lisa is the extrovert, while Iris prefers solitude. Lisa is pursuing law to advocate gay rights activism. Iris is an artist who "feels fortunate to be employed" and takes her career as a professor very seriously. Because both are workaholics, neither is threatened by the other's professional commitments. Their abundant self-confidence frees them to enjoy their differences.

"When you are with someone who is completely different, you double your life experience. Iris is endlessly fascinating to me because of her life history. I get to live the seventies vicariously!"

"Lisa is a lot younger than me, but I feel like I have so much to learn from her. Lisa's Chinese background is absolutely fascinating to me! Her family is terrific."

Iris was a "wild child between the Pill and AIDS," who grew up in a "very German, racist" household in the rural American south.

"My life at home read like something out of Dorothy Allison's *Bastard out of Carolina*."

Lisa, born in Tallahassee, describes herself as "a first generation Chinese girl, surrounded by southern belles—the proper, model, minority American-Chinese kid, who always did her homework and excelled at math and physics."

Iris loves the stability and warmth of Lisa's family, and they were quite taken with her as well. Particularly when, at a family dinner, she deftly used chopsticks to sample the infamously repulsive and

accurately named "Thousand Year Egg." Lisa and Iris have discussed having a traditional Chinese wedding banquet to announce their commitment. Lisa's mother has resigned herself that "all my sons"—including Lisa with her brothers—"are going to marry white girls." She worries that Iris is so attractive that she might leave Lisa for a man.

During the first few months of their relationship, Lisa and Iris were unable to find anything wrong with each other. Once they realized that they had met their match, committing to a long distance relationship was an easy decision.

"You just figure, well, if you've met the right person, then you've met the right person," Iris explains.

So they committed to being together, while being apart. They spend summers together, a month at Christmas, and they try to see each other every four weeks during Lisa's school semesters. Both are too busy between visits to be miserable. They don't see their arrangement as a lesser kind of partnership.

"I think every couple needs to ask themselves, is this the best way for us to structure our relationship?" considers Lisa of the lesbian tendency to bring a U-Haul on the second date. They even think distance may have its advantages. For example, it has certainly forced them to hone their communication skills.

"I think more people should call each other long distance to have some of their discussions!" laughs Lisa.

They have also dealt with the down side—the exhaustion of frequent travel and performance anxiety.

"What if I am not fascinating and charming this weekend?!" Lisa exclaims.

"Or worst of all, what if I don't want to have sex?! But this is going to be it for another four weeks!" laughs Iris.

THE OBVIOUS ISSUE THAT this couple faces is trust. As lesbians, they feel that there is "not a real qualitative difference between being attracted to somebody as a sex partner and being attracted to somebody as a friend. But there is a simple line to draw," says Lisa of their freedom to have crushes. "You just don't engage in inappropriate behavior and that's that."

"Lisa and I decided right in the beginning that we were not going to live for the future," says Iris. "This *is* our relationship. Otherwise, you are living in a fantasy world. Plus, if you start thinking, 'This many years from now, our life, our relationship will begin,' you're throwing away all that time."

"But too many years of this time apart would get old," adds Lisa. "It's like when you run a marathon. You realize that you are only going to be able to make twenty-six miles. It's a great experience, but you don't want to go on for longer than necessary. You just want to finish the marathon. What is important is moving on to something different at different points in your life."

After law school, Lisa hopes to move back to Georgia.

"Queer activists in the south are never at a loss for adventure! It is a very 'front-lines' feeling . . . and you *always* want to be on the front lines!"

"We're seeing it in stages: step one is to get Lisa and me in the same state again; and step two would be to get us in the same house." They'll both do whatever it takes to keep their relationship growing.

"Back when I was still depressed about my breakup with my ex-girlfriend, a real 'cosmic' friend told me to think of my ideal match and 'just put it out in the universe,'" recalls Iris. "I was pretty skeptical, and also still thinking about my previous girlfriend, who was a tall, blonde Danish woman, so I said, 'I want somebody five-four, Asian, and bald!' And that's when I met Lisa. I couldn't find anybody better than Lisa. I wouldn't blow this for anybody or anything. I feel like I can move forward in this relationship, and I don't compromise on that. Even the distance doesn't feel like a compromise. Now that I've known this, I could never go back, but so many people would never even believe that this is possible."

"When I think of commitment I think of partnership," Lisa says. "There's no reason to be committed to somebody unless the two of you together are something more than the parts. When I think about why I feel like I have a strong commitment to Iris, I realize that a lot of it is based on fascination. She's a dynamic person, and we have a dynamic relationship. It is going to be this ever-changing project that we are engaged in. Iris is a creative, interesting person—that's what I am committed to. It's like—let's see what happens now!"

"I think I've really turned a corner in my life," Iris adds. "I used to get involved with people who were morose because I thought they were interesting and mysterious. After all that high drama, this was just so much nicer. Lisa is a real optimist. When I think of all the time that we've spent together, she's been depressed for a total of about fifteen minutes. It is a joy—a relief—for me. I never take this relationship for granted. I just feel so lucky. I don't have good luck really. I never win anything in my life. Lisa's lucky. She says, 'Your luck will change now that you're with me,' and it's true."

"I don't know if this is an ancient Chinese parable or not," laughs Lisa, "but it is better to be lucky than to be anything else."

Karan Ford & Sarah Hryniewicz

"**W**E HAD DECIDED TO LEAVE OUR LIVES," recalls Karan Ford of the momentous decision to retire at thirty-something.

Karan was traveling on business nearly every weekend, and Sarah Hryniewicz worked eighty hours a week at a law firm. They had plenty of money, but no time to enjoy it. They didn't know what they would do, but they wanted to do something different—and not in D.C. Within a week, they had been robbed twice and had their car broken into.

"It was time to get out of Dodge," Sarah says.

They had dreamed of running a bed and breakfast during their retirement. So they were intrigued when a friend told them about an inn that was for sale in Santa Fe, New Mexico. Karan took a detour on a business trip to check it out. It was definitely a "fixer-upper."

"Still, it created a fantasy that I started to live inside of," Karan smiles. "Sarah and I loved the idea of a gay-only property. It was far more attractive to us than doing just plain bed and breakfast work. So it began to spin in our heads."

They took a weekend off in December 1991 to see the inn again. This time, it was "stunning," with all of its flaws now softened by a two-foot blanket of snow. The following August, Sarah and Karan became the proud innkeepers of the Triangle Inn.

They soon discovered the joys of making friends with their guests.

"It is very interesting. At an inn, people ask you lots and lots of personal questions all the time."

Guests always want to know how they got together—Karan says that she had been giving Sarah "lascivious, lip-licking leers" while doing the Tush Push at a lesbian country and western dance.

"Sarah had been involved in this very beige lesbian world, and I was definitely *not* beige!" laughs Karan.

"That's what really attracted me," remembers Sarah. "She was very different from everyone I knew—really high energy, and really enthusiastic about everything."

"Sarah was exactly the same thing for me," says Karan. "She was confident, calm, and serene—that's my nickname for her, Serena. She was just all the things I am not. She was polished, well-bred, and very, very attractive in a cocky kind of know-it-all way. She was just wildly different. It was this wonderful chemistry."

Though they had been casual acquaintances, their first date was nerve-racking.

"I swear to God, I thought I was gonna die. I was *so* nervous. I must've changed my clothes a thousand times. I couldn't even drink during dinner," says Karan. Sarah, too, had to order ginger ale to settle her stomach: "And I don't have any problem drinking! I'm a Polish Puerto-Rican, who lived in Sweden!"

"The other thing that we didn't do," smiles Karan, "is have sex that first night. We weren't intimate beyond normal bounds for a long time. The night that we were first physically intimate, we had dinner at my apartment. I had prepared everything—including crushing green chiles by hand. So we had the hottest sex ever the first time!"

"It still makes me cringe," laughs Sarah.

The other question that guests usually ask them is, "How long have you been together?"

"This question is one of Sarah's personal favorites," sighs Karan. "We have a date we celebrate, but we negotiate on what that is. She always has to tell this story . . ."

"We dated for a couple months, and then she dumped me," Sarah enthusiastically interjects. "She took me out for my birthday for Peking duck. We had a fabulous meal, then she broke up with me; but her credit card was rejected, so I had to pay for the dinner."

In retrospect, both agree that the breakup was the best thing that ever happened. They became friends instead of lovers. But when Karan began seeing a man whom Sarah disliked, she did some hard thinking about what she wanted.

While returning from a visit with him in Los Angeles, Karan says that she had an "epiphany."

"It was that lack of time with Sarah that illuminated what I was missing and wasn't going to get from him." She drove straight from the airport to Sarah's house and said, "We need to talk."

They talked for hours—through that evening, night, and into the next morning.

"It was the kind of conversation that only happens but once in a lifetime," muses Sarah. "We had tried to have that conversation before, with other people in our lives. We shared every secret. We discussed everything. We cried. I'm crying now just talking about it. For me, it was an opening up of the concept that there was a future for us."

"What Karan and I promised ourselves that night was a fifties-style marriage," says Sarah. "We're not going to walk out on it. No one's perfect. No one's going to be the be-all and end-all. We'll just work through it. I think moving to the inn accelerated that process because we were confronted with almost every single issue that couples can possibly be confronted with—all at once. We quit our jobs, moved across the country, started a new business, and went from never seeing each other to working together twenty-four hours a day, seven days a week. With no privacy. It is more work than we thought it would be, because we *didn't* think about it at all. We got here and said, 'Jesus! Who's cleaning the toilets!?' In D.C. I used to boss around a staff of one hundred and twenty, but that didn't work so well with Karan! We went from being executive types to being maids."

"But as it turns out, we love being together!" adds Karan. "We never get tired of that. We enjoy sharing life together and we depend upon each other to make up different pieces of the whole. We are distinctly different in how we react to the outside world. Sarah usually takes a little while to warm up to people, whereas I will even talk to the wall!"

As they intended, the Triangle Inn is only for gay and gay-friendly people.

"We definitely limit our earning potential by doing that," notes Sarah, "but it is very important to us. The more we do this the more we realize how much people appreciate the safety and the comfort level here."

"Our guests don't have to adapt their behavior to make other people comfortable," Karan continues. "We are the self-appointed Gay Chamber of Commerce."

Here couples can celebrate their anniversary with a bottle of champagne, holding hands in the hot tub. When an older woman called to make a reservation, saying her son had stayed there, Karan was up-front with her: "'We are a gay and lesbian property, is that okay with you?' I heard her holler over her shoulder, 'Lewis! They're lesbians. Do you care?'"

He didn't, so they booked the room.

"The inn is not just about being able to create business," Karan states. "It represents an opportunity. We love the fact that we get to live immersed in a gay world. There are lots of gay and lesbian-owned businesses out there. I think that all of us who do this have a commitment to our community—and a joy from caring for the members of our community. We want people to be able to stay at the best place possible and have it still be all gay."

For Karan and Sarah, moving to Santa Fe has been about more than just changing careers.

"We bought a lifestyle. There is life after Corporate America," Karan reflects. "Sarah and I met each other as very thin, very active, very 'East Coast' women. We were sophisticated, city girls with fabulous wardrobes. Now, we wear blue jeans and old sweaters. I don't think that either of us envisioned that we would end up as these soft, chunky, country dykes. Part of the joy of my life is having aged and changed, while still being loved. I have found that there is a road that one travels, and the joy of not doing it alone is immense—and fulfilling."

Pamela Robin Brandt & Lindsy Van Gelder

"THE TWO OF US ARE REAL INTIMACY FREAKS. We push the idea of a lesbian merger as far as we can. For as long as we've been together, it's been a fantasy of ours to be able to live inside the other person's brain," Pam explains.

Lindsy Van Gelder and Pamela Robin Brandt have pursued that ideal for nearly two decades. Not only do they live together, they also work together as co-authors of two books: *Are You Two . . . Together?*, a gay and lesbian travel guide, and *The Girls Next Door: Into the Heart of Lesbian America*.

"Collaborating is an extension of what I like about a merged personal relationship," Pam clarifies.

"I think that when people work together there is a possibility for really transcending what a person can do individually," Lindsy adds. "There is also the possibility for just complete bullshit! We are merged, but in a way we are merged at the throat. We never stop ourselves from arguing. We never hold ourselves back. We always express ourselves. If you squelch the areas where you disagree, you are going to end up giving yourself an ulcer and being dishonest to yourself and to the other person. I don't mean you have to screech really unproductive strings of swear words at each other and throw things and beat each other up. But if you don't have it out, you are more likely to break up than if you do have it out on the table."

Their favorite game is "What Are You Thinking?" The only rule: You must answer truthfully. Not surprisingly, this game often becomes a blood sport.

"We have fought over all the things that people break up over," concedes Pam. "Maybe because we both had early journalism training, I think we are better than most people at thinking about objectivity. So when I am ready to kill Lindsy, I try to look at things from her point of view. It just makes it easier to tell when you are being an asshole."

"WHEN WE WERE THIRTY YEARS OLD, we said that we're going to spend the rest of our lives together, but it wasn't a done deal," Lindsy says. "You don't live happily ever after. You live day by day, and sometimes it lasts. I think that's what people don't see—the constant decisions and work. We decided very early on that we were going to be out of the closet. At the time, it was kind of a radical concept. It made Pam and me

closer—constantly being reminded that this person is so valuable to you that you are willing to put up this fight."

"Honesty is the only ticket," agrees Pam. "Some people think being out is flaunting it, but it is really just being honest about your life. If people want to stay together, they should be out. I really just think being in the closet is an absolute invitation to disaster.

"We began to think of our relationship like it was three people—Lindsy as an individual, me as an individual, and then there was some sort of combination of the two of us that deserved just as much respect. It is very odd to me, how many women are willing to settle for relationships where they can't have the intimacy that women really want. What drew Lindsy and me to each other—and what drew us to being lesbians, because neither of us felt born that way—was that, at a certain point in our lives, it just became so seductive: the idea of having a sexual relationship with your best friend. If you want to sleep with your best friend, it's a lesbian relationship. We are monogamous, but not because we think it is a superior way of life."

"Pam and I are just shallow jealous bitches," says Lindsy, " and we realize that. You have to prioritize what's gonna make you nuts."

"Monogamy or murder—which would be preferable? The answer came to us in a flash."

THOUGH PAM AND LINDSY ARE both Jersey Girls—"It took longer to come out about being from New Jersey than being gay"—they met in New York. "Pam was this rock and roll person. I was sort of a groupie. This is a very odd start to a lifelong relationship," notes Lindsy. "But Pamela just absorbed me. I loved her looks. I just could not get enough of her. I would find all these excuses to be with her. I finally propositioned her and I was so overcome with emotion that my face twitched. I thought this was mortifying, but Pamela liked it. She felt it made me seem sincere."

Pam and Lindsy moved in together in 1978. Pam hated New York and had planned to move, but Lindsy, who had been divorced, was obligated to stay until her children went to college. At the time, they were just four and seven years old. So Pam and Lindsy stayed and raised the children together. "We both felt the other person was worth putting up with things that we never, ever would have chosen on our own."

Lindsy and Pam have finally moved out of New York, to South Beach, Florida; the fulfillment of their fifteen-year-old promise is a compromise between their individual preferences for San Francisco and rural Massachusetts.

Pam and Lindsy have had several commitment ceremonies: a private one at Notre Dame in Paris, one organized by Lindsy's daughters, a group wedding on a cruise to Lesbos, and, of course, the ceremony at the 24-hour computerized Church of Elvis in Portland, Oregon. "We are commitment sluts," Pam says with a laugh.

"Eighteen lesbian-years is like fifty straight-years," cracks Lindsy. "We've had our Golden!"

However, since Lindsy and Pam became a couple, they have never attended a traditional heterosexual wedding and have no intention of doing so—not even for close friends or family—until gay marriages are legalized. "The next wedding we go to is going to be *ours*!"

"BOTH OF US ALWAYS FELT that we were queer long before we were gay," considers Pam. "Both of us were always sort of eccentric. In some ways, it would have been harder for both of us to be straight. A lot of people consider that a disadvantage. They want to fit in. But not me, I have a deathly fear of fitting in—and so does Lindsy. I like the quirky, strange, individualistic aspect of being gay."

"One of the things that's really cool about being a dyke," agrees Lindsy, "is that there's things Pamela can get away with that would probably make me uneasy in a guy—like when she swaggers around like an arrogant asshole. But when she does it, just the fact that she's a woman doing it, it's cool. So I get to like all kinds of politically incorrect things."

"I just love her when she's really *awful*," gasps Pam with obvious relish. "When I used to go out with guys I couldn't stand the idea that they were protecting me on the streets, but when Lindsy and I were first together some guy made a remark to me once in Times Square and Lindsy just turned around and put her cigarette out in his hand. I could *not* believe it! What an asshole!"

"Chivalry is not dead," grins Lindsy.

Pam and Lindsy take genuine—and often perverse—delight in each other's uniqueness: Lindsy likes Pam's green fingernails. Pam likes that Lindsy works in her underwear or "cat-vomity, holey nighties" while writing for the beauty and fashion magazine *Allure*.

"While writing our book we got into this thing that we would take on intermittent butch/femme roles. For example, Lindsy is the Insect Butch because I am scared to death of bugs. So she is the person who always has to kill the insects. And I'm the Power Tools Butch. Well, at least I'm the Power Drill Butch and the Power-Screwdriver Butch . . . "

"Yeah, there are certain appliances that I am the butch of," counters Lindsy.

"When it comes to using the power saw, we have to get an outside butch!" adds Pam.

"And, Pam is the Kitchen Femme. I lost that battle . . . "

Alison Maddex & Camille Paglia

"**W**HAT WE REPRESENT IS A NEW VISION OF the gay world which is more sophisticated—in the gay-male style. Gay men have always been far more successful living as sophisticates in the world, enjoying the arts, enjoying fashion, enjoying living," states Camille Paglia.

Camille and Alison Maddex are enthusiastically dedicated to "all the pleasures of life"—fast cars, the open road, good restaurants, margaritas, smoking cigars, models, movie stars, and glamour.

"We have the same response to things. It was such a relief not to have all this ideology and moralism," says Camille.

"To appreciate television, mass media, and pop culture—not to just critique it but to enjoy it—was a no-no in my field," adds Alison.

Just four years ago, the prospect of finding someone with a similar outlook seemed improbable. Camille had thought the publication of her first book, *Sexual Personae*, would be "the biggest personals ad in the world," thus ending her "ten-year drought."

"I had absolutely no success," remembers Camille. "I was going to lesbian bars regularly, putting my time in dutifully, trying to do the right things. I'm not very good at dating or flirting, I'm afraid. I totally lack talent in that area. It was just terrible."

Subsequent book signings and lectures proved no more profitable.

"I thought, 'Finally these people who really are of similar mind will come to see me.' I was shocked when they did not!"

Although Camille was propositioned, "we weren't quite connecting. People were really down on me, saying, 'You're just too hard to please.' I had basically given up. I accepted my fate. The gods dole out only so much."

But Alison had attended one of her lectures, and began composing a letter to Camille. She didn't know if she was looking for a business partner or a date.

"I was interested in just knowing her," Alison recalls.

Eventually her "application" arrived on Camille's desk.

"Her package had it all! She got it exactly right. It was a wonderful combination of formality and flirtation," exclaims Camille.

Alison's inclusion of her resume established that she wasn't a "crazy person," thereby making Camille's first cut. Photos of Alison's recent artwork impressed her. But, ultimately, it was the picture of Alison bending over in a short skirt that made Camille think, "This is cheeky! This is interesting!"

At their first meeting, they warily eyed each other. Initially, neither

felt the other to be her "type"—until Alison mentioned Saipan. "I had grown up on this Pacific island that no one's ever heard of. But Camille had," Alison explains.

"Something eerie was happening because I knew everything about Saipan," says Camille. "I had pictures of Saipan. I had written letters to Saipan. She'd never met anybody who had heard of Saipan!"

To both of them, this coincidence represented something more.

"SOMETHING IN WOMEN FROM exotic places escapes the Anglo-American conventions. In some weird way," Camille continues, "their experience isn't just multicultural. It was really non-western, tropical, pre-modern, pre- everything! Their experience changes them so that their brains are sort of like mine. They don't have the normal western mindset. I've never lived anywhere but the U.S., but the point is, I've got an odd mind. American thinking is very banal. Every effort of my sixties generation to change it seems to have failed. The banality is a rising tide."

For Camille, who has been the cover story of both *American Jesuit* magazine and *Penthouse,* controversy is fairly standard. Finding someone who shares your views is not.

"I have mixed feelings about this whole gay-marriage thing," muses Alison. "Everyone should have equal rights under the law, period. But I don't know that I want to take on the same ceremonies and contracts as heterosexuals. A lot of those fail. Gay marriage should be something unique."

"Both of us are critical of the direction of gay activism on this,"

Camille says. "We have a more radical attitude, which is a stripping away of the privileges. I want heterosexual marriage not to be given any kind of preferential treatment under the law."

"It's a bias against single people, too. Only children should benefit," continues Alison.

"There has been insufficient research into marriage and what it means," adds Camille. "Civil marriage dates from a period when women didn't have access to careers. It is ridiculous to demand gay marriage in a church or a synagogue. It is ludicrous to demand the approval of a religious tradition that is based on the Bible, which condemns homosexuality. So, we reject the church—and we live our own lives. What our gay organizations, if they were sufficiently intellectual, should be attacking is the whole way the state is still favoring something religious insofar as it says, 'Yes, we recognize a heterosexual marriage, but we don't recognize a gay marriage.' It is a lingering residue of the pre-French Revolution linkage between Judeo-Christianity and the state. The modern state must be absolutely, utterly blind. Everything that gay/queer theory has produced is a crock. The 'social construction of gender' is the way that anxious, weak people have found for dealing with the untidy impulses of their bodies."

With such controversial views, one might assume that Camille receives a lot of negative mail.

"I don't. People are afraid to write to me. They give me a wide berth. They understand correctly that I'm like an unguided missile. When confrontation is necessary, I'm all for confrontation. My whole history is that. But the real revolution is gay people living their lives openly in a way that is *not* confrontational. The real revolutionaries have energy, passion, and are open to the world. I think we have a sense of being role models. It's important to live openly."

"We just act naturally and people treat us naturally," Alison agrees. "We enjoy the company of men. But it is natural for us that we're with women. For me, I don't feel that it is such a political choice. It is just so deep down within me."

Notes Camille, "I said before I met Alison—and people got very mad at me in the gay magazines—that I am not interested in any woman who is not interested in men. That is a symptom of psychological closure. It is very important to me to feel integrated with the world and not to feel embattled. I've heard too often these little formulas, 'men are like this, men are like that.' Give me a break—that's half of the human race. They've invented great art, made the buildings you're sitting in, and made the cars you drive. I really am attracted to men. I am not one of these lesbians who says, 'Eew! We hate penises!' I am very interested in men physically; it's their mental lives that leave me cold. I get along with gay men and straight women."

Professionally, too, Camille and Alison are "totally simpatico." The themes Alison was exploring as an artist/curator were "totally in line" with what Camille was doing in her writing. Now, they collaborate on exhibitions expounding pro-sex, pro-art, pro-beauty feminism. Their professional and personal lives intersect "perfectly."

"The sheer number of things that we are interested in is what drew us together—shared interests, shared tastes, shared sensibility, and humor. To me it is always crucial. I cannot be with anyone who doesn't have a sense of humor, and Alison is extremely funny. Comedy to me is not just fun. It is the enlightened perspective on life."

Neither takes for granted what they have found in each other. "I am Italian. I believe in monogamy. I believe in commitment. I just don't understand the open thing. That is inconceivable to me," says Camille.

"Camille and I are both so independent that there isn't that fear of being alone, but, at the same time, we are not a couple that wants to live apart for long periods of time. We really enjoy being together. I've never felt insecure about this. Not one day. It's not that we're together because we don't know what's out there. We know what's out there, and we choose to be together. As Raquel Welch said to us over dinner one night, 'It's a desert out there, so stay together girls.'"

"And we said, 'If Raquel Welch is saying that to us! Whoa!'" Camille exclaims. "Anyway, I'm more relaxed than I was. I was a maniac in the beginning because I had been *so* unhappy for years."

"I had to kind of beat her back a little! I think we are complementary. The things that I like about Camille," says Alison, "are traits that I prize or don't have. She's very expressive in ways that I'm not. I appreciate that part of her that complements what I have."

"Alison has perfect manners, great social aptitude and judgment. I'm more, 'break through the decorum. Do this and do that.' I'll say, 'You're being too polite. This person is outrageous.' And, she will say 'You're going way overboard.' So, it's perfect."

"I love Camille. People have a distorted picture of her, but I know a very generous, fun, and kind person. I could see a like mind and soul. It was obvious from day one. It just seemed like there would be nothing that I could do that would offend Camille, and nothing that she could do would offend me. We understood each other, period."

"And it was a relief," smiles Camille.

Margarethe Cammermeyer & Diane Divelbess

COLONEL MARGARETHE CAMMERMEYER, PH.D., former Chief Nurse of the Washington National Guard, is the highest-ranking officer ever to be discharged from the United States military for homosexuality.

Though Grethe had struggled with her sexuality all her life, she never thought of herself as a lesbian. When she met Diane Divelbess, however, her life changed in many ways. Grethe and her sons were at their perennial holiday spot on the Oregon coast. Friends were joining them and had invited along Diane, an art professor from southern California. Grethe's children planned to stay up all night on the beach, tending their crab pots. Diane volunteered to keep Grethe company as she watched over them. Grethe played guitar. They cheered the fireworks, ate s'mores and talked all night.

Diane was amazed and enthralled to find Grethe opening up to her; she had been billed as "the Great Silent Wonder." Grethe, too, was astounded to find a listener who made her feel understood.

"I always felt like an outsider; for once I was not fitting into somebody else's mold. I was finally being myself," Grethe reminisces.

They were still deep in conversation when the sun came up. Sadly, that morning Grethe and her boys had to go home to Seattle.

Diane was devastated. "Suddenly, this wonderful woman who seemed like such a good friend was disappearing." In the Portland airport Diane wrote a note thanking Grethe for the weekend. Soon after, there was a reply. Grethe had tried not to think of anything more than "a marvelous evening and Diane as a friend. In the military, you deal with the here and now of life. You don't deal a lot with future things because you never know."

But at the last minute, Grethe had jotted down an invitation for Labor Day on the back of the envelope. They began a long-distance relationship, calling each other every night "to rehash the day."

Grethe and Diane had been together less than a year when Grethe was interviewed to upgrade her security clearance—the next hurdle in her plans for advancement.

"There was a question that came up about my sexual orientation. I had met Diane and didn't want to be blackmailed, so I said, 'I'm a lesbian.' The rest is history," Grethe recalls.

The interview that was scheduled for an hour lasted the whole day. Fortunately, Diane was visiting at the time and was there when Grethe finally came home.

"She looked just like a lump of ash. She told me what she had done and I went, 'The end! How could you be so dumb?!' I was a lesbian forever, so I was used to living in the closet and not feeling bad about that. It was just that there were certain things that you didn't discuss with other people. I could not believe this wonderful naïve burst of honesty. Who goes around telling everyone 'Hello! I'm Grethe. I'm a lesbian!'?"

IN FACT, THIS WAS THE FIRST TIME Grethe had ever used those words with anyone. It was something that she was just beginning to acknowledge herself. Even as a sense of her new identity was emerging, there was a still stronger history compelling her.

"There was every reason to assume, with a twenty-five-year track record in the military, that being honest at that point was certainly what was expected of me as an officer," Grethe explains. "Then to have them say, 'Because of your honesty, we are going to throw you out,' was incongruous. Not only was it very hurtful, it's wrong. So then, it became the challenge."

Virtually overnight Grethe became an activist, a part of the gay and lesbian community that she had known almost nothing about.

"When I first met Grethe, she really, really loved the military that she knew," remembers Diane. "She was an idealistic soldier. You certainly develop a healthy cynicism by being in a university atmosphere, so to run into Grethe was really a breath of fresh air. She was not cynical. She was not used to a wicked sense of irony. She always told the truth. It was something unreal in my experience. So, what I saw happen was that the military by its foolishness in adhering strictly to its own rules lost maybe the best soldier they ever had. Her sense of idealism was shattered. Grethe went in as the Viking Warrior to try to improve them. But her belief in the military went straight down so that the military really lost, lost, lost . . . on all fronts."

Grethe often joked with Diane, "If I hadn't met you, I would have been a general." They had both had serious relationships, but Diane is Grethe's first and only same-sex partner. It was clear from the start that this was a lifetime commitment. For Grethe that was something too precious to sacrifice.

"A meaningful long-term relationship—maybe this is what being gay is all about. I wasn't going to jeopardize that relationship by denying it with the military. If I was going to end up in Washington, D.C., I hoped that I wasn't going to end up there alone. With Diane, everything seems to meld in a very healthy way—not where you are so enmeshed that you don't have individual personalities, but one where you nurture one another to grow and to develop and you feel good. It seems like the right place to be."

"With Grethe, my life has opened to a new chapter which is very refreshing, when you are in a later decade of your life," Diane observes. "You expect things to happen when you are younger. And then, when you settle into a groove and are resigned to a comfortable niche with or without romance—wham-o! everything turns around."

After two and a half years enduring the ordeal of a court martial and her eventual discharge, Grethe began pursuing the case in civil court. Grethe and Diane had to learn quickly how to deal with the constant demands of the media. As more articles began circulating, Grethe decided to write her own memoir before someone else did.

Though Grethe considers her book, *Serving in Silence*, to be a "private conversation," the movie that followed was most assuredly public.

They had been besieged by offers from agents and scriptwriters. One of those calls was from TriStar on behalf of Barbra Streisand. In their first meeting, Grethe was taken aback when Streisand asked, "How do you think you'll like having your life story told on television to millions of people?"

Grethe spoke her sudden realization, "I don't think I'll like that at all." She was reassured, however, by Streisand's conviction that this was the most important social issue of the decade.

GLENN CLOSE WAS CAST as Grethe and Judy Davis played the role of Diane. On many occasions Diane and Grethe had to remind themselves that it was not really "our movie." They laugh about a scene in which they have an argument. "Grethe and I don't fight!" But they were told that in a love story there has to be a reconciliation. At other times, the production seemed so true to their lives they felt as if they had been spied on. During filming, Grethe found it too painful to watch some of the clips, particularly of the interrogation scene.

Serving in Silence ran during sweeps week and won, with 25 million viewers. Later it was awarded three Emmy Awards, including Best Actress for Glenn Close's performance, and a Peabody Award. Grethe and Diane laugh now, remembering how nervous NBC was about sponsors. "This was in February of 1995. Now, if there's no gay character on television, it's like you are out to lunch."

Grethe and Diane pursued the "bizarre experience" of having their life made into a movie because they recognized that their story was the medium for the message.

"We were characters," Grethe explains, "but the purpose of the movie was not to tell about our lives, it was to talk about the issue. The central message was that gays and lesbians have lives and families, people who care. They fear for and lose their jobs. They have to deal with the stereotypes and prejudice. The movie was trying to take those stereotypes that we have been raised with and ask questions about them. To have those questions in people's homes is valuable."

"WITHOUT THE RELATIONSHIP," considers Grethe, "I don't know if I would have been able to withstand the onslaught. Two minds are better than one sometimes. Because of Diane's personality, there is a sense of coming home to calm. Diane was always there and continues to be."

"I have always been in awe of Grethe's strength of purpose, her endurance, her ability to 'put up with,' and to do it so well," declares Diane. "She doesn't just stagger through the day. She triumphs."

Grethe won her civil case and was reinstated. Though she is now retired, the battle is not over.

"I was not doing this because of my case." Grethe's words are as thoughtful and measured as her resolute gaze. "It was the principle that this was a very unjust policy and I was naïve enough to think that they would see the error of their ways and change. You have to fight to make these things go away or they just continue to stack up. As long as someone is willing to listen, my job is to continue to speak."

Gwen English & Monna O'Brien

THE VERY FIRST TIME THAT MONNA O'BRIEN ever set foot in a gay bar, she met Gwen English. Gwen was approaching her thirty-fifth birthday, and Monna was just twenty-five. Gwen, who was put off by the age difference, remembers driving down Lakeshore Drive with Monna's blonde hair flying and bare feet sticking out the window of Gwen's Cadillac Seville.

"Monna was so light-hearted and playful. She just drew me to her. She was fresh air. I looked at Monna and said, 'You are going to be difficult, but I'll give it a shot.'"

"I loved that Gwen was so different from me," Monna says. "She was so comfortable in her skin. She is who she is. Gwen means what she says and says what she means. It was very different from anyone I had known. It is something that I still admire about her."

They had been together only a few weeks, when the difference that was at first attractive became overwhelming. Monna had always dreamt in color. Now, suddenly, her dreams were monochromatic—all blue, all green. Color became significant as she considered her life with a person of a different race.

"I had never been with a black person. I was absolutely terrified," recalls Monna.

For a week, Gwen watched Monna withdraw, and then she confronted her. "Look, here are your choices—you can go backward or you can go forward—but you cannot stand in the middle. I think that your best choice is to go forward, but you have to make that decision. I will not stand for anything else."

Monna made her choice—and she and Gwen have been moving forward together ever since. But the path that they have chosen has not always been easy.

Six years into their relationship, Gwen had a mid-life crisis. She was "downsized" twice. Each time, it took nearly a year to find another job. At the same time, Monna's career was taking off.

"It was so confusing to me. It was never about who she was—I was so proud of her. It was all about 'where the hell am I?' I felt as if I still had a lot to offer, yet wherever I was making those offerings, I was being turned back."

Year after year, Gwen struggled to find some direction. Finally, in their twelfth year together, the pressure became overwhelming. As a result of the stress, Monna began to experience physical pain. Her knees were aching so severely that she could no longer get in and out of a chair. Monna tried orthopedics, acupuncture, physical

therapy—all with no effect. Then she had a realization.

"My knees hurt because of where Gwen and I were. It was like my feet were in cement. It was not going to change until I changed the things that were wrong in my life."

She went home and told Gwen, "You are unhappy here, and I am unhappy here. It is time for you to go."

Gwen moved out that day.

"Something drastic had to happen to get us out of the stuck place that we were in," Monna explains.

They continued to talk and to go to therapy. Though Monna had doubts, Gwen saw beyond their immediate situation.

"IT WAS LIKE A FOG HAD LIFTED. I could see my life more clearly. I didn't know what was going to happen, but I was just unwilling to allow what we had together as partners and lovers to be destroyed by the circumstances of our lives. These things should not be what would destroy us. If this relationship is going to end, it is going to end because we don't want to be together anymore. Because I don't love Monna and Monna doesn't love me. It was not going to end because of those things that are a part of living every day. I felt that we had it in us to work through those things. They only took time."

They were apart for six months, during which time Gwen began to work on a Ph.D. in clinical psychology.

"That was what turned things around for us. When Gwen became happy with her life and loved what she was doing, then we could become equals again. Gwen became a partner to me. One of the things that makes our relationship work is the passion that we have for our lives. The passion between us never went away. It was only that we didn't individually have passions for our lives."

They have not had a crisis of that magnitude in their relationship since, but almost from the start they have had to press onward against an undercurrent of disapproval.

Gwen had already been with Monna for five years when she came out to her mother, who simply asked, "Are you happy?" then added, "Did you think I would love you any less?"

Monna did not have a similar experience. Her parents were outraged. They didn't expect her to be gay—and certainly didn't expect her to have a relationship with someone of a different race. The more upsetting of the two, they always say, is that Gwen is black.

"It's been a long, hard road with my family." Monna was, in fact, disowned for a time. Then the situation was not discussed for years. For both women, it was devastating.

"I had not personally experienced prejudice," Gwen says with shock and disbelief. "It was the first time that I had ever had that kind of hatred directed toward me—simply because of the color of my skin. They didn't know me. They barely knew my name."

Monna was heartbroken. She not only loves her parents. She likes and admires them. In the moment of their rejection, all her worst fears came true.

"I am willing to take the lack of acceptance by the rest of the world, but that I couldn't find safety in my family has been a really hard thing for me. They still can't say, 'I gave my daughter the strength to establish a relationship that is strong, true, and as committed as any relationship ever has been.' I see that it really was a gift that they gave me. It saddens me that they can't see the value in it. It saddens me that I can't share this joy."

But Monna has again come to a realization.

"It has been a very hard thing for me to constantly be in the position of having to choose between my lover and my family. It ought not to be a choice. The most hurtful thing that I have done to Gwen is not take a stand with my family about the relationship. All the way around, it was a mistake. I fault myself a lot." As Monna continues to stand by the decision she made all those years ago, to move forward, with Gwen, her family, too, is making small but hopeful steps toward acceptance.

THE BOND THAT HAS KEPT Gwen and Monna together through everything is their appreciation of being loved for who they are, not who they are expected to be.

"One of the things that I valued most about Gwen—and still do to this day—is that Gwen loves me unconditionally. It was so freeing to me and felt so good."

"Why is it that we don't just throw up our hands?" asks Gwen. "I just love Monna. I love her a lot. I like spending time with her. I like my life with her."

"Gwen and I feel that we share intimacy at a level that is beyond the physical. We are emotionally and spiritually intimate. This rela-

tionship has given me a spot to feel safe, so that I've been able to grow. What I always say about Gwen is that she holds my heart, but she holds it very loosely. She always allows me to move forward and has never held me back from anything. I am a very determined person," says Monna. "I had always seen my life in terms of being committed to another person. I knew that I loved Gwen and that this relationship was something that I wanted for the rest of my life."

THEY HAVE COME TO SEE the day-to-day workings of a relationship as simply a series of conversations and interpretations between two people. When there is conflict, "either I am not telling her right, or she is not hearing it." They have decided not to spend any of their conversations in conflict over past struggles. They don't want to waste the time they have. Throughout their relationship, Gwen and Monna have lost many friends to AIDS and other illnesses. Those experiences have clarified their commitment.

"It has served to continually illustrate to us what are the valuable things in life. It comes down to the happiness that you find—and those that you love." Monna reflects on all the eulogies that they have written, and pauses to consider how they themselves would like to be remembered.

"If all that anyone said is that we loved each other well, I would be happy. I think that is a pretty good tribute. It is a very lucky thing to find someone to love. It's a gift."

Shellie Collier & Shely Landsberger

JUDGING FROM THE DOZENS OF SNAPSHOTS THAT overflow shoe boxes and tumble out of cookie tins, Shellie Collier and Shely Landsberger's relationship seemingly revolves around parties and friends, and plenty of both. They are laughing at the camera in photo after photo—poolside at the Dinah Shore golf tournament, dancing with friends. Everyone in every shot is beautiful and tanned; the picture of health, portraits of their prime.

There haven't been too many pictures like that recently. Not in the last year. Not since Shely started to lose weight and get headaches so severe that she couldn't see clearly enough to drive. Then, she began to have blackouts and seizures.

Shely and Shellie had to wait a week for Shely to get an MRI. During that week, Shellie had a recurring dream—they were in a hospital with someone walking down a long hallway toward them. In her dream, she knew that the moment of truth would be whether this person spoke to Shely first or to her. If the person approached Shely saying, "Can we see you," it would be good news; but if the person turned to Shellie and said "Can we see you," it would be the worst news imaginable. When the day finally came, it was just like her dream.

"I heard the door close and footsteps coming down the hall. That must have been the longest two seconds *of my life!* I watch him. He's coming toward me, with his mouth open. Then, he says to me, 'Can we see you?'"

Shellie enters a room where three doctors are waiting and she thinks "Oh my God! Please don't say what your faces look like." They told her to sit down.

"I don't need to sit down, just tell me what it is."

"She has a tumor—very large."

"What does that mean?!"

"Very, very, very large."

"All of a sudden," Shellie remembers, "I feel like the floor is gone. I don't even know how I am standing. I don't know what the fuck has just happened to my world."

The doctor says, "We should decide what to tell her."

Shellie is confused, "What do you mean 'decide what I am going to tell her'? I'm going to tell her the *truth*!"

"We don't always recommend that."

"You know what? I've never lied to this woman a day in my life. I won't start now." Shellie walks into the examining room where a panicked Shely is furious after the long wait. One look at Shellie's face—and Shely knows.

"What is it?" Still, she asks Shellie.

"It is a tumor. It's a brain tumor. What do you want to do?"

"Well," Shely responds, "I think that we need to go have a drink and a cigarette."

T HAT DAY WAS MARCH 12, 1996 —and nothing has been the same since. The tumor was discovered to be malignant and inoperable. One day Shely was working, the next she wasn't. Now, Shely, only thirty-three-years old, is making daily trips to the doctor for radiation and chemotherapy. Her plans are on hold and projects sit unfinished in their garage. Shellie won't complete them without Shely. She is waiting for her to feel well again. Shellie is working to support both of them now, so friends have formed a volunteer rotation to help out. Shellie and Shely can't thank them enough—not for the practical help or for "the hugs and the 'I love you's.'" The whole situation still seems surreal to Shely. "I'd never been sick or taken prescription medicine before. I'd never been in the hospital. When my hair fell out the first time, it became a little bit more real."

Shely's outlook on life has changed as a result of all that she has experienced. "Every once in a while we cry. It's a little bit scary when you read the statistics about brain tumors. They're really bad—some of the worst percentages of all cancer. I've heard a million times, 'Oh my God, I would never have the strength that you have. You have so much courage.' I respond, 'You would *too*! I guarantee you.' The

strength was so automatic. It was like taking a deep breath," Shely describes. "You believe that everything happens for a reason—that it happens for the right reason."

For Shellie and Shely, the reason is love. They have found something in themselves and in their relationship that they might otherwise never have realized.

"It taught us what true unconditional love is. No matter what the outcome, we'll always feel blessed that we had true love."

Trust and compassion, like their love, are not just abstract ideals, they have been forged into actions that are lived out daily, hourly. "It is a different kind of trust—not hoping, but knowing," Shellie explains.

"There is no escape hatch. I am very grateful to have someone like Shellie beside me. I know that I am going to be with this person till the day I die. Even though I know that I am going to beat this thing that is in my head—the idea that I would be leaving Shellie behind is definitely a driving force to fight it. Not being with Shellie is hardly something that I can think about. Under any circumstances, I would support her and defend her. There is not anything that would make me leave her and not love her."

"For me, the day that I realized that I unconditionally love Shely was when I discovered that all of Shely's faults that used to irritate me were now something that I loved about her. Now when Shely feels irritated about something, my new response is 'What can I do to make her not feel like this?'"

"The things that we used to bicker about, all those things went away. The true kindness and importance of each other's love, the appreciation, was the whole focal point," Shely clarifies.

SHELLIE AND SHELY have been together five years. The relationship has matured, suddenly and cataclysmically, to a point that is "beyond words now." Their life in the photo albums seems a lifetime away. For Shely and Shellie, there are no more late night parties and no more strenuous activities, but there are also no resentments.

"At first, I tried to go ahead, do things, and make an appearance for the two of us. It was the most lonely time of my life. I couldn't stand it! I would much rather be with Shely, just lying with her. It's enough. It doesn't matter if this is what our life is going to be like for the next eighty years—I still feel extremely fortunate. She is the most trustworthy, passionate, and compassionate person that I know. Her loyalty is undying. Those things, in a million years, I could never repay." With Shely, Shellie has glimpsed a vision that infuses her with hope. She has experienced a love which is "powerful and will move mountains. I am beyond thankful and grateful that I've had the chance to know what unconditional love truly means. I am humbled that I have received this gift. What keeps me going, what keeps me from being consumed by remorse or bitterness is that—I've had it for a moment. From the moment that I saw Shely, I never had eyes for anybody else. There was just something beyond the physical presence, we saw into the future. We knew that we would spend the rest of our lives together—that we would have houses and children together. We always knew that the last time we ever saw each other would be when one of us buried the other. What makes me know that we are going to get through this is that I saw us when we were older—having a life together. We are going to make it through this."

Stella Guillen & Linda Velasques

Stella Guillen and Linda Velasques became friends in the sixth grade. They were just twelve years old. By the time they turned sixteen, they realized that their attachment was romantic.

"It just happened," remembers Linda. "Stella made me laugh. I liked being around her. I just couldn't wait till the next time I saw her. It was just that special feeling. It doesn't matter whether it is a girl or a boy, when you fall in love with the person. It had to be what everybody was talking about—true love."

More than two decades later, these childhood sweethearts have been together longer than any other couple in both their families.

"To me, it was a marriage. It was now and forever, and that's it," says Linda. "Either we do it for good, or we don't do it at all."

"I had lots of apprehensions," admits Stella. "We're talking about Texas in the mid-seventies. I just didn't know what we were going to have to face in the world. We've had to make a lot of decisions every day, every week, and every year that we've been together. I think we made the right decisions all along."

Stella and Linda's approach to staying together is simple, but not easy. "Trust," Linda states in one word. "It was the one thing that Stella emphasized at the beginning. She said, 'I don't tolerate lying,' and I said, 'I wasn't raised to lie, so that shouldn't be a problem.'"

"One of the successes of our relationship is that we have always surrounded ourselves with family," adds Stella. "I bet we had lived together four or five years before we even knew there was a big gay community in Houston."

"We were brought up with the same values, traditions, and religion—the same faith and the same loyalty," agrees a smiling Linda.

Stella and Linda have been a couple for all of their adult lives. Tears well up in their eyes as they talk about growing up together, how far they have come, and how much they have loved each other all those years.

"It was before acceptance and openness about coming out to your families," says Stella. "It was before all that became chic or popular. I'm not saying that we are trendsetters or anything like that. I just mean it, with everything in my heart, when I say that Linda was honest from the beginning and held me to it. With Linda, I've always felt good, important. I've felt a part of something. We are a team, a couple. I couldn't ask for anything more."

LaVerne Harvey & Teresa Walker

BARE-LEGGED AND BAREFOOT, ELEVEN-YEAR-OLD Teresa came running into the store.

"Mister, Mister, do you have any carpet for my fort?"

"Oh my God, she's so cute!" LaVerne said to her husband. "Who is she?"

She was his niece, Teresa Walker. LaVerne Harvey was only seventeen years old herself, when she married a man who had a drinking problem and a nasty temper.

Though Ocala is not a big place, LaVerne and Teresa didn't have much to do with each other during the next eight years. LaVerne managed in her marriage—and Teresa grew up.

In August of 1980, LaVerne came home from the hospital with her third child, having hemorrhaged so badly that she could hardly walk. While her husband was off on a bender, LaVerne needed help, and Teresa stepped in to help during her time of need.

"Hardly knowing me, she looked after me like a baby," LaVerne remembers.

Teresa became her live-in nursemaid, though they had been virtual strangers. LaVerne found herself wanting to be with Teresa constantly. She was jealous of Teresa's friends. She followed her around.

She felt like she was falling in love. And Teresa was feeling the same.

Each thought it was her own little secret until, one night, they had a fight. It started with thrown beer, turned into a roadside scuffle, and ended with LaVerne being thrown in a ditch full of water—but not before Teresa suddenly kissed her.

LaVerne slapped her across the face and yelled, "Don't you ever kiss me! I'm not a lesbian!"

Teresa assumed she would move out that night, but LaVerne stopped her.

"Don't leave. I think you love me. I think this is what it is. You love me, and I love you. But I'm sure there's a mistake here because we're both female—and what can women do?" LaVerne asked.

From then on, every morning after LaVerne's husband left, LaVerne and Teresa would lay in bed "and be secretly close—we'd discuss in depth what this meant." They wrote each other notes and letters trying to figure out their feelings. They would probably have gone on like that for sometime if LaVerne's husband hadn't come home unexpectedly and seen them through the window kissing.

"He was drunk and went berserk. It was scary," LaVerne recalls.

As Teresa ran out, LaVerne decided that she was finally leaving too. As soon as she stepped out the door, her husband attacked her, ripping her clothes.

Pushing her to the ground, he hissed in her ear, "If you stay, nobody will ever know—but if you go, everybody will know."

They escaped; and he stayed up all night calling every friend and relative, turning them against LaVerne and Teresa.

They had nowhere to go, so they moved into a trailer and got jobs as carpenters' helpers.

"You couldn't 've gotten no poorer than us. There were a lot of nights we didn't eat 'cause we fed the kids," remembers LaVerne.

MEANWHILE, LAVERNE'S HUSBAND stalked them. He watched them from his car. He repeatedly sent social services to question them and would sometimes call the police with trumped-up complaints. He wanted to stir up trouble for them—in whatever way he could.

"I was so fearful that they would take my kids away. We lived like we were just best friends all those years," says LaVerne.

He often phoned in the middle of the night screaming.

LaVerne remembers one threatening call in particular in which he yelled, "I called the Marion County Sheriff's department, and they told me that I could kill you because you are a lesbian!"

"It was like me and her against the world I'm telling ya," LaVerne explains. "Everybody turned their backs on us. We even questioned ourselves. We didn't know any lesbians. Were we really going to go to hell forever? I don't even know why Teresa stayed. She had to have been crazy. I was just madly in love with her."

"What made me stay?" Teresa responds, "I loved her. I just thought that, if we could escape everybody and get around positive people, it would get better."

And it did. When LaVerne's ex-husband had their Pinto repossessed, it gave her an idea.

"I thought that this repo man must make money. I knew that I could repossess cars—and not be mean like that. I wanted to do it," LaVerne says.

After having the repo man arrested for assault and battery, they went to every car lot that he had worked for, claiming to be repossessors. Finally, they got a bite.

"If you can repossess this one car, you can have all our business," said one dealer. The car that they had to repossess belonged to a professional boxer—an ex-con who had beaten a man to death at the Red Rooster bar. They asked around and, in only forty-five minutes, had his address in Jacksonville, Florida.

They spent their last $140 on a used Datsun—its hood was held down with stereo-wire, it took more oil than gas, and it had a leak in the tank so it only held two dollars worth of gas at a time. "It was basically a bomb!" It took them six hours to make the one-hundred-mile trip to Jacksonville.

"With girls doing it, they never had a clue. They would just tell you everything," Teresa proudly remembers.

The police had been looking for the ex-con for six months. LaVerne and Teresa found him in one night.

"And that's how we started our career," grins LaVerne.

Teresa and LaVerne have been in the business for the last ten years. When they first got a little money together, they moved out of the trailer and into a mobile home.

"I don't think I've ever been so proud of anything in my whole life. It is a wonderful feeling to earn something like that," reflects Teresa.

Now Teresa and LaVerne are living in their second new home and own their own car lot. And they still repossess cars.

"Back in the beginning, we just stole all of them. We didn't realize how dangerous that was. LaVerne would go right up in the middle of a drug bust and take a car," marvels Teresa.

"Teresa can pop a lock faster 'n you can put a key in and turn it," counters LaVerne.

They have seen their share of sticky situations, including being shot at. Teresa remembers the first time that they hot-wired a car.

"I knew half from watching *Starsky and Hutch*, and LaVerne knew the other half. We messed around a little—and cranked that baby up! What we have learned to do, we learned together. Everything that we have done, we've done it together for the first time. Lord help anybody that tries to get between us. I don't care who it is, I stick up for LaVerne one hundred percent, even if she's wrong—that's not the point!"

"There is no such thing as compromise in love," states LaVerne. "Somebody has to give in and that's that. If you compromise, then neither one of you is happy. One of you has to allow the other one to be happy. With Teresa's love, there is literally nothing that is too much to ask of her. I like the fact that when I can't go anymore, Teresa has ten miles left in her. I like having somebody who's always on my side. We've always been there for each other—always. I get so mad at people thinking because you're together a long time that means you don't care anymore. I'm majorly attracted to Teresa. I think more attracted now than ever. Can you imagine the hours we have spent together? I still get real depressed if I have to spend a whole day alone. If she even gets up and leaves before I get up, I'm upset."

"If I go to work without her, I can't wait to get home—just to see her," Teresa nods. "I love everything about LaVerne. She is my life."

"Before Teresa I had no life. It was like she saved me. Teresa gave me *me* on top of giving me her. I remember the first time we walked into a gay bar. We were *amazed*! There must've been six hundred women—dancin', drinkin', laughin'. We just followed everybody around, listening in on their conversations and watchin' 'em. We had no idea.

"Back then, you really thought you couldn't be anything or do anything without a man. We both started out on the bottom. Everything that we have now, we made together," grins LaVerne. "The best revenge is living well."

Diane Racine & Kimi Racine

AFTER SPENDING ONLY A WEEK'S VACATION IN Provincetown on Cape Cod, Kimi and Diane Racine decided to move there.

"We woke up the second morning of our vacation, looked outside, and said, 'We could wake up here every morning. What are we waiting for?'" Kimi remembers.

Friends thought their plan to relocate in six months was crazy. They were back on the Cape in three. They quit their jobs in Portland, Oregon sold their house, transferred their son, Brandon, out of school, and drove three states a day. They arrived with no jobs and no place to live.

"Fear is lack of faith," says Diane. "You just gotta do it."

Now Diane drives for a laundry service, and Kimi waits tables at the Lobster Pot. They are happily settled into their new life. In the gay enclave of Provincetown, Kimi says that they don't have to "spend energy fighting against people who tell me that it is not okay for me to be who I am." Instead it takes them two hours just to walk down Main Street; every few feet they stop to visit with friends. On the wall of Brandon's fifth grade classroom hangs his drawing of his family. "I was born in Portland, Oregon. My Mom's name is Kimi. I like to play baseball and hockey. My other mom's name is Diane." For them, living in Provincetown is about being part of a community. Diane has been elected vice-president of the PTA: a big step for someone who was at first hesitant to get involved with a woman with a child—a child who grew up calling her '"Honey" because he thought that was her name.

"PEOPLE SAY THAT THERE'S one right person out there for you. I think that there's probably a million and that you could make any one of those work. To be in a life-long relationship," Diane believes, "both people have to want to make it work. Both people have to be willing to continue to grow inside the relationship. You have to be committed to it, you have to be willing to work on it, and you have to be willing to change together. When you say 'till death do us part,' it's not, 'I don't think I like this anymore, this is not feeling good, I'm outta here.' Kimi and I have probably had that thought pass through our brains a million times, but we don't leave."

"I remember," Kimi says, "the first time Diane said, 'You know, I'm not going anywhere,' meaning that whatever you end up going through, and whatever you end up feeling, even if there's some ramifications, I'm still gonna be here. It's not the easy answer. It's not about 'be nice, compromise, be romantic,'—all those things that you would think. It's about, 'communicate and don't go anywhere.' When we haven't been able to communicate, we've still been able to trust in the process.

"People are amazed that, if I am attracted to somebody else, I will tell Diane. It takes the power out of it because it is only in my head. I think that anybody can make it through the honeymoon stage and a lot of people can do the next year-and-a-half of compromise, but that is when you start identifying what it is that you want and what you are willing to do to get there. At that point, you dig deeper, get more intimate, and find something new. You can do it if you want to. You just have to want to. You have to know that this is where you want to be."

"Some people get into a relationship," adds Diane, "and think that it's going to look, feel, and sound the same way from now until whenever—and it just doesn't. I know that whatever is making me happy today in this relationship or in my life may not be what makes me happy tomorrow. You hold onto things so tight in your life that you strangle them."

Kimi agrees, "You have to be willing not only to listen to your partner, but to open up yourself. Each of us is a whole lot different than we were eight years ago, or even different than we were a month ago. Every time I change, if I am not willing to share with Diane what's going on with me and bring her into it, she is on the outside. You have to continue to keep the lines open and be honest about who you are, what you like, and what you don't like."

"WHAT I WANT IN MY LIFE is to be settled down," Diane declares. "I want to come home and know that somebody is going to be there—we are going to go shopping together, to the movies together, to *live* together. Gays are afraid to take anything from heterosexual relationships, and it is true that because we are two women living together the emotional attachment and sensitivity are totally different, but I know that my mother and father have loved each other for more than forty years. They stick with one another no matter what. If you are not willing to look at a heterosexual lifestyle and say, 'I can have the same happinesses and joys and togetherness that they have,' then you have nowhere to go. We have to get rid of that internalized homophobia—all of the stereotypes that we have about ourselves. As a community of lesbian people, we have to start figuring out how to honor ourselves and to know the happinesses, joys, and togetherness that the rest of the world enjoys—that we can have every bit of that and it doesn't have to be the same, but it doesn't have to be different.

"IT IS ABOUT MAKING the commitment to be with one person," adds Kimi. "I don't label myself anything, necessarily, but what I know is that when I met Diane—if Diane was a man, I could have just as easily fallen in love with *him* too. Because when I fell in love with Diane I fell in love with the person that she is. So whether or not in the past or the present I am ever attracted to men, that still does not make me bisexual, because I am only having sex with one person—that's her. I always tell people I didn't stop having sex with men because I didn't enjoy it, I stopped having sex with everybody except Diane because I am in a monogamous relationship with her. I made a joke once about divorce, and Brandon right away said, 'You guys are fine! I don't know what you are talking about— we're a family! Is this gonna be like *Mrs. Doubtfire*?!"

That story still makes them both laugh. "We talk to him about us being grandparents for his kids, about supporting us when we get older. We always tell him he has to go to college and get a good job," laughs Diane, "and he'll say, 'I'll go to college, but you guys still have to work!"

KIMI AND DIANE are not afraid of hard work. They have both struggled successfully to overcome drug and alcohol addictions. They have done the therapeutic work necessary to heal childhood sexual abuse. They know who they are and where they want to be, and with a good measure of faith they will get there.

"Our latest journey is to reclaim our heritage. I'm Hawaiian-Korean and Diane is French Canadian-Native American, but we were both brought up white. It is part of a passion that we both have to identify ourselves as women of color now," Kimi describes.

"It is a very important thing that gets lost and causes your spirit not to be settled, and when that happens it is really hard to be a whole person," adds Diane.

ON THE DAY THAT Kimi and Diane took the same name, exchanged their vows, and committed to being a family together, Diane says, "something inside of me changed. It blew me away. I had always been a 'transient lesbian': two years, you're outta here! All of a sudden with Kimi we are pushing three years, four years . . . eleven years! We are breaking new ground. I think that's the reason that we continuously get different heights of awareness of one another. We all of a sudden wake up one morning and say 'God! I really love you!' I think that you get to a different level and end up falling in love with that person at that time."

"It is just amazing and better than the honeymoon stage because I know Diane so much better and I know myself so much better. I know more today what this is really about. Because of that sense of commitment that we have, we could pick up right now and move someplace else. We have one another and Brandon—no matter where we go, we will be okay."

Vinnie Levin & Kristi Parker

SHORTLY AFTER MOVING TO WICHITA, KANSAS, Sharon "Vinnie" Levin met Kristi Parker. She had heard about Kristi's newspaper, and took every opportunity to suggest a collaboration.

"I annoyed the hell out of her. In a lot of ways, Kristi is a purely cerebral person. And I am a purely emotional person. I was very pushy. I had this very strong belief that I could make her paper excellent. It was already good, but I knew I could tip the scales on *The Liberty Press*. I had this passion for it. I just wanted it really, really bad. I can't say that I had ever thought that I would want to spend twenty-four hours a day with someone, but from the second I met Kristi, I always wanted to be next to her."

"It happened just like everybody always tells you," smiles Kristi. "I was completely and totally comfortable being single. When you quit looking, somebody pops up. I always knew I was never going to be able to stay with somebody who couldn't keep up with me—intelligence-wise, work-wise, humor-wise. Vinnie really is the first person I've ever met who challenged me.

"She really scared me. She was so aggressive and pushy. It seemed like she wanted to take over. But there were so many things

that I wanted to do. I had all these ideas, and it wasn't until Vinnie came along that we really started implementing them. We could stay up as late and work as often as we wanted." *The Liberty Press* is now Kansas's longest running lesbian-gay newsmagazine.

"People expect a difference about our relationship because we are in Kansas," says Kristi. "I don't think we treat our relationship any differently. Sometimes, it is not until Vinnie points it out that I am ever aware that we are breaking new ground. People are their own worst enemy—far worse than anybody else."

"Kristi has taught me just everything about being out," adds Vinnie, "about truly being comfortable with yourself, being comfortable with your partner, and really being gay all the time. I wish that I could tell everybody else how wonderful it is to be out. It's not as hard here as everyone thinks." Vinnie and Kristi plan to make their lives together in Wichita. Vinnie proposed a permanent collaboration.

"I found somebody that I can look at every single day and fall in love with," Vinnie smiles. "I've always been capable of these really big emotions. Most of my life I've spent thinking about them, knowing that they could exist. Now I've settled down. I'm just so happy. I really feel like I have another half."

TJet Clark & Julie Tolentino

"A LOT OF PEOPLE HAD SAID TO BOTH OF US about the other, 'You're just gonna love this girl,'" TJet Clark recounts.

"And they were right!" Julie Tolentino smiles at TJet.

"I was doing tech work on a show that Julie was in," TJet recalls. "When I first saw her, I thought that she was amazingly beautiful."

"We started out just being friends, with absolutely no commitment," remembers Julie. "I wanted to make sure that I didn't disappoint her. I kept asking, 'Do you want something from me?' And she said the most amazing thing that to this day still touches my heart, 'I want exactly what you have to offer.'"

TJet is a construction worker and runway model for Calvin Klein. Julie is a professional dancer and, since 1990, has run the Clit Club, a lesbian dance club, in New York City. They now work together on that venture as well as on other projects.

"We live very rigorous day-in, day-out lives," Julie explains.

"We spend all this time together in work-mode, so we have to remind ourselves about our relationship time. We have that time on what we call Saturday," TJet says with a smile. "After the club closes, we come home at 5 A.M.—at the earliest. The rest of the day

is just ours. If the phone rings, we don't answer it."

Their time together is special because they truly enjoy each other's company.

"TJet likes me for all the things that most people hate about me," observes Julie. "My problem areas, it turns out, are all things that TJet loves—my neurosis about my body, my nervous moments. She even thinks that it is interesting when I am awkward. She is able to appreciate these parts of me that I've either fiercely held on to or tried to hide. I actually accept myself in a different way now because of her appreciation of me. I have never before felt like I could say that someone absolutely wants *me*. Ultimately, she taught me how to give that kind of love and openness. She certainly has blessed me with that."

"I lived many years as an unlovable person," says TJet. "I had a fifteen-year heroin addiction. When I met Julie, who had everything going on, I realized that she was the kind of person that I used to fear because she might recognize that I didn't want to get my shit together. In so many ways, she has taught me what it really means to make a commitment. We always say to each other, 'You give me courage.' Courage and encouragement are so much the same. And she backed it up. It wasn't just a moment or something that she just

said. You can go home with somebody that you don't know and feel those things, but to be able to wake up and look at yourself and this other person everyday, that is what we hope for in everyday life. She's the one. I love her, and I want her to like me. The truth is, to like someone is a harder thing than love. We continually say, 'You are my best friend.' And we mean it. It isn't just a catchphrase for us. Strangers can say, 'You look great,' or 'You did a great job,' and it just sort of goes in and comes out. But when the person you respect most on the planet tells you that you are okay and things are going well, it feels *good*. Since I have pride in this relationship, I have more pride in myself. I spend a lot of time alone because I do construction work in empty apartments. Throughout the day, Julie's there in my thoughts. When I met Julie I thought, 'Julie is really, really cool. I like her so much.' There's not a lot of people in relationships who can say they really like being with their partner, like doing things with them. I'm so proud that she wants to be my friend."

"OUR FRIENDSHIP ISN'T JUST sisterhood, we lust after each other!" exclaims Julie. "We had crushes on each other. We were jumping around like two little girls, saying things like, 'Wow, this is amazing. You have the best skin. You have the most amazing touch. I can't believe that your feet look like that.' All the beauties that come in the beginning were there. But somehow we connected beyond an aesthetic. The way that TJet sees the world is what interests me the most—the way she articulates what she sees and the way that she is in the world. I am absolutely fascinated by all those aspects. That is why I am in love with her. I welcome the interesting or intriguing or beautiful women who pique TJet's interest. However she deals with that is just part of me experiencing TJet. It is part of her doing her thing, it is part of being TJet. In a relationship, I am not going to ask you to pardon me, to look away at certain moments and take me only at the right moments. You lose those aspects of self in monogamy."

"We have a very open relationship in all aspects of 'open,'" adds TJet, "and it is about wanting as much for someone else as we want for our own selves."

"The truth is that every once in a while a really cute little girl comes along and my mind goes wandering," agrees Julie. "And we like those parts of each other. No one enjoys, experiences, or gets to have anything that goes on between TJet and I. I don't *expect* to be everything to her although I *am* everything to her, and TJet is everything to me. I trust TJet like I've never trusted anyone, not a family member, not another friend . . ."

"She'll say, 'Do I look fat?' If she does, I'll say, 'Yeah,'" quips TJet.

"That's how I knew for sure that she was the right one!" Julie laughs. "But that's the thing! I can rely on her honesty. It really challenges me to be that honest. I couldn't do anything without this kind of relationship that I have. The reason that I can do what I do and have the courage to be creative is that I am really not alone."

Natasha Eastman & Gold Wilkerson

HEN NATASHA EASTMAN JOINED GOLD Wilkerson's company as her trainee, something unusual happened.

"I started to feel a little tingly," Natasha recalls. "I always heard stories of falling in love—the bells and the fireworks. But I was a skeptic because it had never happened to me—much less with a woman. My heart would pound every time I saw her. I had never felt that excitement before, that rush when you saw a person. I went through a few torturous weeks. I wasn't even sure she was gay. I would try to figure out from her hairstyle because I read books that said that gay people wear their hair a certain way! She had me a total wreck. One day, I decided that I had to confront her."

At first, Gold was shocked. "But, three months later I realized, 'Wow, you're attracted to this woman as well. Go out and get to know her. She's wonderful to be around. She's a gorgeous woman.' I adore her. But what really clinched it was her kids."

Natasha is the mother of two daughters, aged six and eight.

"I feel that children are a reflection of their parents. As a single mom, Natasha was just fabulous—incredible. I just took to the kids. I fell in love instantly. I've gotten lucky here, blessed. I think that sub-consciously I examined how committed Natasha was to her kids because I felt that if she didn't love the kids she might not love me. For most of our relationship, I have been in the hospital because I have degenerative bone disease. When we initially met, I was preparing for major surgery. Once I was back on my feet and ready to go back to work, I got hit by a van, so I was back in the hospital again! But every day that I looked up, Natasha was there for me."

It was worth the wait, they both believe, for what was meant to be.

"I've always wanted to be married," considers Natasha. "I've been engaged twice, but they were not the right people. I haven't always seen Gold with my eyes, but I've always seen her with my heart. We couldn't be any other way. What I've found in this relationship is everything that you read about in romance novels and see in Cary Grant movies. I have my own Waltons mixed with the Brady Bunch thing—except that it doesn't end in half an hour! I see us growing old together, having grandchildren, doing the Labor Day barbecue and the whole nine yards. We have the love. We have the children. We have the commitment. All that we need is the house with the white picket fence! But I feel that we're very rich. We have an overflowing abundance of what really matters in life."

Judy Nelson & Kay Pfaltz

O N A SUNNY SUNDAY AFTERNOON, A GROUP gathered at the local polo field in Charlottesville, Virginia. Judy Nelson had come to play, and Kay Pfaltz to watch. They noticed each other before the match, and lingered afterward to talk—though neither recalls a single word of that conversation. They both agree that it was love at first sight.

"We just knew," Kay remembers. "I can't stress that enough—because I've never felt that before. People know when they are attracted to each other. We all have that. Oftentimes, it is mutual—but this was something different. I felt really confident that this was *it*."

Judy Nelson has thought a lot about the subject of love. She has written two books, *Love Match* and *Choices*, that chronicle her very public love life. She first came to prominence in her hometown of Fort Worth, Texas, as a national beauty queen, the Maid of Cotton. At twenty-two, she married her college sweetheart. For seventeen years, she lived a life of country clubs and motherhood. As her marriage slowly dissolved in the face of her husband's infidelities, she met the tennis star Martina Navratilova. At the age of thirty-eight, Judy was as surprised as anyone to discover that she was in love with a woman. She made the difficult decision to join Martina on tour and was immediately immersed in the nomadic and demanding world of professional sports.

Judy and Martina had been called the lesbian version of Marilyn Monroe and Joe DiMaggio. They were partners for nearly eight years before the relationship ended in 1991. Judy was once again in the spotlight, this time not as a celebrated beauty or a celebrity lesbian, but as a litigant in defense of what she felt were her rights as a spouse. In a much-publicized lawsuit, Judy took Martina to court over a "non-marital cohabitation agreement." Though they later settled privately, the recriminations were rancorous and public. Judy only just found peace and contentment when she met Kay.

"In mid-life, I've found myself really looking at my life, as a lot of women do. That was difficult for me. We were always taught that fifty is old—when you live your life based on your looks especially. It's taken me all this time to go full circle—back to what I feel is really important. I'm much different than I was when I was younger. I think that is probably why Kay came into my life at that time. I was at a place where I didn't feel that I had to have somebody in my life. Kay had been at that point much longer than me."

"I had been alone for so long," Kay explains, "in New York,

London, Paris—those big cities make you feel lonely. At first, it was what I wanted. I wanted to be out on my own, to do my own thing. I lived alone for ten years. I was okay, but I started to want somebody for myself. I wanted to be part of a couple more than anything in the world. I just wanted someone to brush my teeth with. In an affair, you don't have that. You have very high moments of passion and romance, but you don't come home to the day-to-day stuff. When the Martina-Judy lawsuit was going on, I never knew about it because I was in France. I picked up her first book in a bookstore in Charlottesville, and thought, 'Gosh, she's pretty, I'd like to meet her.'"

Now, two years after their first meeting, Kay and Judy are busy putting the finishing touches on their renovated farmhouse, Big Willow Farm, near Nellysford, Virginia. Kay, a private person, describes Judy as "the talker," and says that their relationship is "everything I always wanted."

THOUGH FALLING IN LOVE came easily, their commitment to one another was a conscious effort

"Both of us were wise enough to realize that we needed to go back and lay some groundwork," recalls Judy. "I was going through a lot turning fifty. Kay is younger than me. There were so many things that had to be looked at. We felt it should work because our hearts said so. Our souls matched. We felt that connection, but just feeling those things is not enough. I would insist that couples look at that. It's not just about 'oh boy, this feels so good and so right. This is my soul mate.' Hey, wait a minute, that's all well and good—those pretty little words—but you've got to be with that

pretty little person when they are not pretty, when they make huge mistakes, and when they make little bitty ones that just tick you off. We spent a lot of time putting that foundation together and finding a way to make it work for both of us—and to nurture the relationship as well."

"The highest compliment that I can pay someone is to say they make me laugh," smiles Kay. "And you know, Judy does that without even trying! Judy is the most important person in my life. Love is one-on-one. I think we all want to be number one for somebody."

"I think that it is innate in all of us to want to be in couples, to love and be loved," agrees Judy. "Kay gives me this real sense of calm."

"Our relationship is also very passionate," adds Kay, "which is something both Judy and I need."

"That is one of those things," Judy says, "the minute you say 'passionate' and you are in a homosexual relationship everyone is, 'Oh my God! I don't wanna hear it!' I think one of the big fears people have is that if we talk about our relationships in a positive way we will influence their children about a lifestyle they don't want for their children. As a mother, I can understand that they want better for their children than they had it. They want it easier for their children than it was for them. Because of the choices I've made, yes, sure it's made some things difficult for my family, for my kids and probably there is no greater regret that I have. None. The vicious cycle there, of course, is that if there were no prejudices, if *everyone* would get over their own prejudices, then life would not be hard for anyone!"

KAY AND JUDY ARE HAPPY living in Nellysford. Rudy, their seventy-year-old neighbor, drops by with peaches for them. Others shovel their lane when it snows. Here, in the poorest county in the state, everybody helps everybody else, "they just stop and do."

"I think that we're accepted here," says Kay, "because they know us on this individual basis. They might say, 'Ya know, I'm against homosexuality, but Judy Nelson's okay. She's real sweet!'"

Kay grew up nearby, and Judy is a self-described "good southern woman" from way back. "I realize that sometimes when I open my mouth I am going to make waves, but I hope they are gentle ones," Judy explains. "I would like to see change but I want to do it in such a way that you don't really know that it is happening. Change is like growing old; it should be a comfortable process that enriches your life."

They talk about "getting back to basics." They believe in the sanctity of marriage and that a child requires two parents.

"Children need one-on-one nurturing," Judy exclaims. "I don't care whether it's from a mother and a daddy, two women, two men, two monkeys! It doesn't matter." For them, "family values" are simply about valuing family.

On August 11, 1996, in a Romanesque church in the south of France—just as Judy and Kay had always wanted—they had a commitment ceremony reminiscent of a traditional wedding. As they exchanged vows, *Ave Maria* played in the background. When the ceremony was over, the church bells rang to sound their celebration.

"I think if you don't have similarity in your backgrounds then you fall apart rather than falling together," says Judy. "I never looked at that with my spouses. But I looked at that with Kay and knew there was a common ground there."

"I never thought that I'd be happy again in the United States," says Kay. "I would have chosen to make my home in Europe if I had not met Judy. But I am completely happy here. We each love the country. We want to stay here forever."

"It is about pace, a sort of cadence that goes along with breathing. People from the cities would think that we lived this very affluent life," Judy smiles, "when in reality it is a very hands-on way to live. Maybe what is so appealing about all this for us is that we do have the little bitty grocery stores where they know your name. If you don't have enough change, you can pay the grocer the next time that you come in. There is something very appealing about that. It is about trust. It is what we need to remember in all that we do. I found that this is my peace. I am perfectly happy to be in the city with all the lights, the hubbub and all that, but I only like it for about three days at a time. Then I really want to come back here, put on my jeans that I've had for seventeen years, and just 'be.'"

JUDY AND KAY FEEL NO DISTINCTION from their neighbors. When the world wakes them from their idyll they are all the more incredulous.

"Why do they need to think, 'Oh! I can't imagine myself being with a woman!'" Judy shakes her head in frustration. "What difference does it make?! On a real level, it doesn't matter, so why do we at some point make it matter? Take ten heterosexual couples, they

probably make love ten different ways. So it is not about that. Liberty and the pursuit of happiness is right there in the Bill of Rights! Why then, am I, because I choose to be with a woman, being excluded? It blows me away, that I don't have and am not protected by the same freedoms as everyone else in this country. I'm not hurting anybody. I remember living at a time when interracial marriages were illegal.

"At some point we will have the same freedoms as everyone else because that is what our country was founded upon. I remember my son Ed telling me when he was twelve that one day he would be president of the United States, and I remember that shortly after I had chosen to spend my life with a woman, he was certain that I had changed things for him and that he could never be president because who would vote for a president that had a lesbian for a mother. He was probably right, ya know. So I've decided then maybe I'll just have to be the first lesbian that becomes president! It is not about writing letters to your representatives. It is not about leaving it up to somebody else and hoping they make laws for us. It's about going out and getting elected and making our own laws. Then we'll make a difference. 'Come out' is a very foreign term to both of us. I didn't feel like I was 'in' anything! For us it is a matter of just living. It is really just coming forward and saying, 'Hey, this is who I am, this is how I live. I'd like you to meet Kay, this is who I love.' It doesn't matter how we got here. Everybody's path is different. Whether you think you were born gay, or by some social structure you got that way, or it's a choice to be gay—who the hell cares? The point is—I love Kay. She's warm, tender, and wonderful. We have the qualities that I really desire in a relationship. Now, if that makes me a lesbian, then that's what I am. But I can stand here and say that I am *not* any different today when I tell my family that I am in love with a woman than I was the day I went to my parents and told them I was in love with a man. It is no different. The feelings are the same. I am the same person. My values are the same. Love, honesty, trust, and commitment are as fundamentally important as they always were. I'm proud of who I am. I'm proud of who I love. There are lots of women out there like me. There are lots of women out there like Kay. There are lots of couples like us. You just don't know who they are."

Diane Israel & Ivette Visbal

DIANE ISRAEL AND IVETTE VISBAL ARE PROOF that opposites attract.

Diane, a native New Yorker, was a Nike-sponsored professional triathlete and distance runner who competed in the Iron Man and other competitions around the world before becoming a therapist. She describes herself as "hyperactive" and is often up at dawn for the first of her two daily workouts.

Originally from Colombia, Ivette is a high school Spanish teacher. She is laid-back and mellow. Ivette claims that "the pace in America is a little faster than I can do." She misses the Colombian traditions of siesta and long, drawn-out dinners. For Ivette, eating is a pleasure, not a source of anxiety.

"She'll have mocha with whipped cream, and chocolate cake with ice cream," laughs Diane. "Just being with her, I've become more free."

Fortunately, they have at least one thing in common—they both moved to Boulder, Colorado, in the eighties.

Despite their differences in personalities, the relationship is calm and stable. Sometimes, they worry that it is too much so.

"Our biggest challenge is keeping the romantic, sexual, and inti-mate piece alive," notes Diane. "Both of us had been involved in volatile, tumultuous relationships in the past. When Ivette and I met, there was a different feeling. There was a groundedness and a health-fulness to our relationship. I think that it has made us question sometimes if there is enough fire and passion here. I know that we have tremendous respect and amazing love for each other, but it is not that 'movie love'—hot and heavy—though we do have moments of that. I'm a thrill seeker. I live on adrenaline. When you come from something that is more up and down, and dysfunctional, not only do you get conditioned to the volatility, but you might get somewhat addicted to it. Ivette will say things like, 'Let's be grateful that every-thing is going so well and everything is so smooth and calm.' There is a part of me that completely agrees with that—and then there is a part of me that says, 'Yeah, but what about the excitement?!'

"Our commitment parallels the differences of who we are as people. Where Ivette is slow, steady, predictable, and stable, I am a little wishy-washy, more impulsive, and less secure. More than Ivette, I question things. I need to be liked, to fit in. Sometimes, being a les-bian feels really isolated—I start thinking that maybe I would be happier if I was with a man and we had a family. I bought into that.

Then, I project that this relationship isn't okay, and that I need to leave to find something else. With all these secrets that I had in my head, all of this confusion, it was like this whole other relationship that I was having with myself that Ivette didn't know about. So now I am putting things out there even if it is really scary. I want to be truthful. The most truthful I can possibly be is in the moment. There is not a day that goes by that I don't let Ivette know how much I care about her. I adore Ivette. I love Ivette. She is already enlightened. She doesn't have to go looking for it. Ivette is my Rock of Gibraltar."

"You chose to be with a certain person because that person is ultimately good for you," Ivette declares. "I wouldn't be in a relationship simply because I am good for that person. There has to be a lot that comes back to me. Diane is very sensitive, sweet, respectful, loving. She is very accepting. She loves all people. She is the most non-judgmental person that I have ever met. Diane is very innocent. She has opened up a whole new world for me that I did not know. It wasn't a very happy experience for me in Colombia.

"I knew since I was a teenager that I was more attracted to women," Ivette continues. "I can't even call this a choice. It just came to me when I was young. I superficially came out to one of my best friends that I had a crush on, and she had a fit. Before I was able to finish my sentence, she said, 'I hope you're not telling me that you are a lesbian?' That was the end of my trying to come out to anyone. I did briefly think about taking my life. I go back to Colombia every year, but in Colombia, half of what I say is a lie—because this is half my life. Here, I have the freedom to be myself. In Latin America, in relation to the whole homosexuality issue, there is a lot of ignorance.

My mom is a wonderful mom, a beautiful mom, but I moved here and chose to stay here because I will never forget my mom saying to me, 'I would prefer to have a daughter who was a prostitute than a lesbian.' It did not sound weird back there and in that context, but it has always stayed with me."

"Ivette is really courageous," says Diane. "She is committed to being with me through all that she has to put up with. It gives me strength in getting through the hard times, when I doubt, when I feel the discomfort of being with women."

THEY HAVE COME TO EXPECT the freedom and tolerance that they have found in their relationship and in the United States.

Ivette once eschewed all things "feminine"—makeup, high-heels, dresses. "For a while, it almost became a uniform. All lesbians had to look a certain way. If you didn't look that way, then you didn't belong. That is a generalization that I don't want to engage in any longer. It is okay to feel attractive. It is okay to do things to yourself that attract other people. I don't always want to worry about how much of it was invented by men."

"I have always prided myself on androgyny in terms of wanting to celebrate feminine and masculine," adds Diane. "Being the adolescent that I forever am, I rebel. I would love to see the stereotypes broken. If every lesbian wants to judge me because I am a 'straight lesbian' they can. And I have been judged that way. 'Oh, she's definitely going to end up with men.' I would love to see all lesbians who feel like it just be more feminine than the typical heterosexual woman. Go the other way, choose to be with a woman who can appreciate fluffiness and ballerina outfits. I happen to appreciate it when people think I am attractive."

Ivette and Diane embrace a world that is "more than just us." Ivette says that they would like to see the lesbian community "go beyond the politics to a place where we can become less judgmental and homophobic of each other."

Diane and Ivette are nonconformists. They don't want everyone to be the same. They don't even want to be the same as each other.

"I love variety," says Ivette. "I don't have to be with a person who is just like me. It would drive me crazy. I would get bored to death. The wonderful thing about our differences is that Diane and I give each other the space we need."

"I couldn't classify myself truly as any label," says Diane. "That's not my nature. As long as I can be a woman and show my love to Ivette and have it be real and authentic, I don't think the label is what it is about. Any category takes away from human potential. The way we are really going to impact the planet is people being okay with 'self'—whatever that is. Why not have the sky be the limit in possibilities and potentials? Why not open the lens as wide as possible rather than cut ourselves short? It is possible to question—break the stereotypes—to really be free."

Carol Iwata & Judith Niemi

"IN THE 1970S, IF YOU THOUGHT SOMETHING should happen, you just did it. There was this wonderful, creative, 'we will change the world by next week' feeling," Judith Niemi remembers.

In this spirit, Judith started her Minnesota-based company Women in the Wilderness, an outdoor education and adventure travel organization for women only. On a canoe trip, she met Carol Iwata.

"Canoeing together is one of our most active and tangible ways of being partners," says Carol. "We don't have to say anything. We can read each other's motions. It is an extension of the way that we are in our everyday lives. There really aren't models for how lesbians should have relationships, so you figure it out as you go along."

"It doesn't feel like Carol and I ever said that we are in a capital 'R' relationship," adds Judith. "We never sat down and defined rules about it. We don't use words like spouse or marriage. I am not looking for a blessing from Washington, thank you."

Moving in together was admitting that they had become serious.

"But the two of us could not discuss things like that for a long time," allows Judith. "We both have to remind ourselves sometimes that it is okay to talk about this stuff, because we weren't brought up that way—neither the Finns nor the Japanese are let-it-all-hang-out kind of people. We don't always say a lot about what is going on, but over the years I really have learned that I can say anything to Carol. There is nothing that we can't talk about. When you are younger, you look around for what is a perfect fit. There aren't any perfect fits."

Though Judith and Carol consider their relationship the primary one in their lives, they have also "spent time" with others.

"So-called infidelity is not a capital offense in our relationship," explains Carol, "but lying would be very close to that. Part of how Judith and I work our relationship is that we are honest. These phases of 'non-monogamy' have been our 'growth experiences.' They certainly have forced us to muddle through to ever-increasing clarity about what is really central to our relationship—what our relationship is really about. I love Judith because she is wild and funny—and open to trying lots of things. I would trust my life to her, and I feel that she brings that out in me."

"Being trusted is a real gift. Carol grounds me. She is somebody whom I can absolutely count on. We don't say 'forever.' It is not part of our vocabulary, but I think that we have decided that we are permanent."

Eva Antonijevic & Mandy Wheelwright

ONE OF MANDY WHEELWRIGHT AND EVA Antonijevic's prized possessions is a binder filled with letters from friends and family. The letters describe "a devoted couple, productive in their work, engaged in the world and supported by a loving circle of friends." They tell of a "storybook romance," that is the object of envy and respect.

Interspersed are photographs and notes sent between Eva and Mandy, but it is not just a scrapbook of keepsakes and remembrances. The binder is neatly organized with dividers and headings. At the front, a letter from their lawyer is addressed to Canadian Immigration. The binder is Mandy and Eva's proof that they are a committed couple. It is their application to be allowed to remain together in Canada.

MANDY AND EVA MET IN 1983 when they were both working at Fenwick's, a London department store, during the Christmas rush. Mandy heard Eva's "amazing accent" in the staff cafeteria. They spoke and later ran into each other on the Tube.

"I had just graduated from university in Canada," recalls Mandy. "My parents were from Britain, and I had dual citizenship. So I thought that I would try my luck in London."

"I was born in Slovenia," explains Eva. "I was nineteen when I decided that I couldn't stay there any more. I already knew a little bit of English, so I went to England."

"It just feels like there's been such extraordinary circumstances that brought us together," considers Mandy. "I think that it has to be about some connection that is bigger than just your everyday run-of-the-mill bumping into someone."

They felt the same "amazing connection" in their growing feelings toward each other.

"To me, it is less about gender, and more about the individual you are with," says Mandy.

"I think there's a spectrum," Eva agrees. "There's total homosexuality on one side, and total heterosexuality on the other. Then there's people in between. I've had relationships with women before, but, because I was brought up in Eastern Europe, I thought that, though being with women was fun, you just had to get married and have children. Everyone does that.

"I still feel that our London time is the foundation of our relationship. We really just had each other," says Eva.

Mandy worked freelance for the BBC and Channel 4, and Eva became a stewardess with British Airways. But eventually, it was time for a change.

"Sometimes, relationships break when two people have different ideas. We somehow always change at the same time," says Eva. "We support each other's dreams. We feel very important to each other. Because we have this connection, all other things are easier. We don't even think of it as a compromise."

While Mandy was missing Canada and wanting to broaden her career, Eva decided to quit the airline and go back to school.

"Eva is truly from a socialist country because she tends to work in five-year plans!" laughs Mandy.

They had visited Mandy's home town, Vancouver, and considered it to be "half-way between Slovenia and London." Eva got a student visa and enrolled as a biology major. They settled into a home and put down roots.

"But every six months to a year, when I went to renew my visa," Eva recalls, "there would be some person there who had just finished university—and was getting thrown out of the country. It was painful to watch. I knew that eventually I would graduate and face the same problem. What were we going to do?"

At the same time, LEGIT, a lesbian and gay task force, had started the process of applying for landed immigrant status for same-sex couples under the Humanitarian and Compassionate Grounds clause, a Canadian immigration law originally intended to help people bring over their maiden aunts and other relatives. It was, in effect, a discretionary policy that broadened the definition of family. With the help of LEGIT, Eva and Mandy were one of the first couples to apply for residency under this provision.

"We had to show that we are emotionally, economically, and psychologically interdependent. Because we live in a compulsory heterosexual world, all those questions were not foreign," notes Eva.

"The big question," adds Mandy, "was—and it was stated quite clearly in the interview—Do you consider your relationship equal to that of a marriage? We obviously answered in the affirmative. But, the real questions are: Who is defining marriage? What's a good marriage? What's a bad marriage? What's a real marriage? And what is a false marriage? Why aren't common-law heterosexual relationships valid? The definitions that we have of family don't relate to society very well anymore. We should redefine family as people who live interdependently."

"We are like opposite parts of each other," smiles Eva. "I am more emotional, impulsive, and compulsive where Mandy is more balanced. On the other hand, I make Mandy move a bit. We definitely complement each other. That is the bottom line. Especially now. After you hit thirty, the time just goes—like that. It is scary! We find each other a real comfort."

"And I never run out of conversation with Eva. We always have things to talk about. We are always on a similar wavelength," adds Mandy.

MARRIED COUPLES NEVER HAVE to demonstrate their attachment to each other by meeting the same burden of proof that Mandy and Eva have had to defend. To prove their interdepence, Mandy and Eva compiled their wills and their financial records as evidence. To show that they had been together a decade, they had to find old envelopes postmarked 1983 that were addressed jointly. They were asked to write personal essays about what each means to the other, and to have family and friends write letters describing their relationship.

"It felt like a bizarre thing to ask people to do, to comment on a relationship that was so personal," Mandy quietly remarks.

"It was like washing laundry in public. You had to totally expose yourself," Eva adds.

They have mixed feelings about the intrusiveness of the process, but certain letters and essays are very special to them, including a poem that Mandy's mom submitted and a hand-written letter from a neighborhood child as well as their personal essays.

After a tense waiting period, they received official notification that their petition was successful on Valentine's Day, 1993. Eva was granted landed immigrant status on the basis of the nature and duration of her relationship with Mandy.

"We know what we mean to each other," says Eva. "We don't need a ceremony. But this put a seal on it. If anything, this had a strengthening effect. It made us think about it—"

"—and articulate it," finishes Mandy.

"It is a celebratory, watershed moment for our relationship."

"WHAT MANDY MEANS TO ME: *Mandy is as important to me as the air I breathe. It is a miracle that we ever met; two people from opposite sides of the world meeting somewhere in the middle. It is unnerving to think what would become of my life without her, my soul mate. The void and the longing in me would be unendurable. I love our life together. I treasure and appreciate what we have. I often joke that in this age of addictions, mine is Mandy. I need her so deeply there is no cure or remedy but large daily doses of her. My analogy for our life is that we are two vines and our love is a strong, high wall which supports us and allows us to grow all intertwined and higher and higher so we can bloom in different yet complementary colors."*

"WHAT EVA MEANS TO ME: *Eva is my lifelong companion, my lover and my very best friend. I feel very lucky to have found such love and companionship which I know is rare. I was searching for compatibility and equality, for someone who was willing to give as much as they took. When I found this ideal in Eva, it was like the missing piece of the puzzle all of a sudden falling into place. I feel closer to her than anyone else I have ever known. I cannot express my feelings for Eva enough even if I were to write a hundred pages. We have a life and home together. It is an integral part of why we feel so happy, productive and secure in the world. This home is now Canada."*

Lynda Roth & Muffin Spencer-Devlin

MUFFIN SPENCER-DEVLIN IS THE FIRST PLAYER in the history of the Ladies Professional Golf Association to declare that she is gay. Muffin didn't come out to become golf's lesbian spokesperson. She did it to relieve herself of the burden of keeping secrets. She did it because she wanted to hug and kiss her partner at the end of her next tournament win. She did it because she was in love with Lynda Roth.

Before they were a couple, Muffin and Lynda were friends. Professionally, they are well-matched. Lynda is a composer who works in film and television. Consequently they understand the weight of performance and the erratic roller coaster of success. But "life's ups and downs" has a different meaning for Muffin—she has been dealing with recurring bouts of manic depression since 1974.

"At the end of my third year in college, I had a manic episode and was diagnosed," Muffin recalls. "I went through about five years of trying to figure out how to deal with that. I decided that I wanted to play golf as a way to put discipline in my life. I tried playing golf while taking lithium and anti-depressants, but my fine motor skills were impaired."

Throughout the eighties, Muffin successfully treated herself with diet and a vitamin program. But she suffered a relapse in 1990.

"It is not something that you necessarily heal from. It is something that you have to deal with for the rest of your life."

During her first LPGA press interview, Muffin talked openly about her struggle. "It has never been something that I have hidden," Muffin claims. "I just hoped that somebody would pick up the paper and think, 'I'm a manic depressive too and here's somebody who has succeeded with manic depression.' The stigma busting of mental illness for sixteen years prepared me for coming out as a lesbian. It was—and remains—important for me to be able to express who I am and not pretend to be something that I am not."

Lynda, too, grew up with a sense of difference. Hers was the only Jewish family in a small town outside Pittsburgh.

"I didn't even know what a Jewish American Princess was until I went to college in Boston. I've already dealt with being a minority, so what else is new?" Lynda quips.

FOR BOTH WOMEN, being a lesbian couple is secondary to just simply being a couple, working through life's adversity together. On May 19, 1996, they had their own marriage

ceremony in a park near their home, surrounded by a circle of more than one hundred friends and family. Lynda, who previously had been opposed to gay marriage, found the exchange of vows profound.

"It was the most euphoric experience of my life. I was very surprised. No one I knew who had ever been married—gay or straight—had ever said to me that you feel euphoria. Everyone said that you get nervous or cold feet."

"I was in the depressive part of the illness, not being motivated or taking the initiative," Muffin shares. "The really incredible thing for me about the day itself was that I was able to rise up out of the depth of the depression to really experience the love, the joy, and the euphoria. It was a truly joyful experience for me. About a month later, I came out of the depression fully and began to feel like myself again."

The first four years of their relationship had been "like a honeymoon," according to Lynda.

But, when Muffin became more frequently depressed, Lynda too found herself "in a shadow place."

"I am a 'rescuer.' I don't want to be the rescuer. I don't want to have to keep taking care of Muffin—and yet Muffin is used to being taken care of. Subconsciously, we all want the status quo."

They started going to couples therapy. For Lynda, it was a novelty.

"Friends said, 'God, a Jewish woman who hasn't been in therapy! What's wrong with you?'" Lynda laughs. She likened the experience to "being in a canoe going down the rapids! Most people I know don't go through this stuff. They do their trade-offs—even if it doesn't make them happy, they say, 'Well, I'll give that up, I won't fulfill that part of myself, I better not rock the boat here.' In our parents' generation, they didn't even get to think about that stuff. They were raising kids and were in their roles. It is a blessing and a curse that we have chosen the path to know ourselves. Growth is painful. It is so overwhelming. It makes me feel honestly that, for the first time since we've been married, our relationship is finally realistic. This is what a relationship is about. Of course, a lot of bubbles are burst. We are, as a society, under a grand illusion of what relationships and true love are about. When the natural issues of any human relationship come up, people think, 'Gee what happened to that magic we had?' They get scared and run away from that."

Muffin and Lynda have learned that love itself can be transformed. They have discovered a new kind of love—different from the romance of the honeymoon period.

"Muffin and I grew through romantic love by having our wedding. The next stage of commitment is working toward 'Agape,' this place of a higher love, where, through compassion, we honor each other as individuals. We knew nothing about this place when we met each other."

"We have grown through the wounds of childhood to functioning adults," adds Muffin. "We do not try to fix one another, but support one another in our individual life's work, as well as our life together as a couple. It now becomes clear to me that I have to fix myself. That is a bit of a scary proposition. Intellectually, I am clear that it is an important part of healing for me; but at a gut level it seems over-whelming. Coming to accept that responsibility is a big part of the battle. It is a much safer feeling to be in a relationship while I struggle through the depression. Because of Lynda's understanding and compassion, my journey through the illness has been—if it is at all possible to be positive—a lot more positive than it ever was in the past. I feel understood. During the years of our friendship, Lynda made a conscious decision to be in a relationship with someone who is manic depressive. Certainly, no one ever before went out and did any homework."

For Lynda, being with Muffin is an inspiration.

"I had a lot of respect for how Muffin kept bouncing back. She just wouldn't throw in the towel and give up. The work that we are doing is scary, but we are not running away from it. The act of working through it one day at a time sometimes seems like such an upward climb. It is so new. I've never experienced this with anyone. Despite all my associated feelings of fear, I grow individually as I realize the positive aspect of my feelings—my love for Muffin. I do have compassion for Muffin, and I want to learn more about that. I believe in Muffin, even when she disappoints me. It's not about her living up to my expectations. It is about my belief in her spirit. Now, to me, the chance to believe in her goes way beyond romantic love. It is the chance to really honor someone else's spirit and soul—to build a life based on that."

Phyllis Lyon & Del Martin

"THE FIRST TIME THAT I SAW DEL, SHE HAD ON a gabardine suit and heels and was carrying a briefcase. I had never seen a woman carry a briefcase before. I was impressed!" Phyllis Lyon remembers.

Little did Del Martin and Phyllis know that this meeting would be the beginning of a forty-five-year-plus relationship. In 1950, Phyllis was working in Seattle for a trade publication when Del was hired to come up from San Francisco. Phyllis threw a welcome party for Del, who spent most of the evening in the kitchen—with the boys—smoking cigars and trying to learn how to tie a tie. "We all thought that was a little strange but not terribly."

The next day, Phyllis recalls, a hungover Del called, disgruntled to learn that she couldn't get a drink in Seattle on a Sunday. When Phyllis invited her over for one, they struck up a friendship.

Then one night at a tavern, Del remembers that she, Phyllis, and a friend were talking. "Somehow or other—none of us can remember how—but the subject of homosexuality came up. They wondered how come I knew so much about it, and I said because I am one!"

Phyllis thought this was intriguing.

"I was curious as heck! I really liked her a lot and I pondered and pondered. My first awareness of homosexuality was in high school, because a classmate, a young man who'd been in the same drama class as me, committed suicide. I cannot remember anything that was said, but somehow or other I knew it was because he was—I don't know if I knew the word—'queer.' I thought that it was so awful, a loss. I never heard the word lesbian until I was in my twenties—when Del said it!"

Phyllis and Del's relationship began on Valentine's Day in 1953.

"We were the first people to have that as an anniversary. Now everybody has it!" exclaims Phyllis.

They got an apartment, planned a move to New York, found a house in San Francisco instead, and have lived there ever since 1955.

They concede their first year together was "traumatic." It was difficult making the transition from independence to togetherness. Del insisted that they open a joint checking account immediately, which made Phyllis antsy.

"But we did it anyway," Del smiles.

They have made every purchase together ever since. Once, during a fight, they burst into laughter at the same time.

"It was just so ridiculous! I finally said to Del that we were going to stay together for a year if it killed us. Then we couldn't split up anyhow—because we didn't know how to divide the cat!"

In the early days, Phyllis thought that any woman wearing a Pendleton jacket was a lesbian.

"What did I know?!" Phyllis laughs. "But then, you didn't dare ask at that time. It was especially hard for us to meet lesbians because we were too shy to talk to the ones that we did find—the ones that were in bars and so on. We just sat and looked at them and wished. It seems weird now!"

Finally, they were introduced to another lesbian who knew of six others who wanted to form a secret lesbian club, Daughters of Bilitis.

"Would we be interested? We jumped at the chance. More lesbians!" Finally, Del and Phyllis had found a community in which they could truly be a couple. Daughters of Bilitis was "a coming out place," a place for lesbians to build self-esteem.

"Back in the fifties, we certainly didn't have any," notes Del. "We were considered illegal, immoral, and sick. That's a lot to deal with. So we had to build acceptance. We were okay, no matter what other people thought."

By 1960, the club had chapters nationwide and had become the first lesbian political organization. Del and Phyllis also co-founded a newsletter that turned into the national magazine, *The Ladder*.

"We didn't have a large subscription list, but we had a large readership! If they all had subscribed, we would have been in a lot better shape!" laughs Del. "Back in those days nobody talked about sexuality, let alone homosexuality. We didn't have the vocabulary to even look it up—what we were feeling—in a dictionary or the library." When Del and Phyllis's own book, *Lesbian Woman*, was published in 1972, libraries couldn't keep it on the shelf because people too embarrassed to sign it out simply stole it.

Del and Phyllis's lifetime of "abundant voluntarism" in the gay and lesbian movement began with the idea of eliminating the anti-gay sex laws. "We've done that in more than twenty-five states!" Phyllis proudly says.

BUT THEN, AS DEL AND PHYLLIS would remind you, they have always been political and pride themselves on their shared backgrounds. Both are journalists. Both are lifetime Democrats, active in the party. Both grew up in the Depression era and were deeply influenced by Roosevelt. And both feel firmly that they would not have made the gains they have without their involvement in mainstream politics.

All those years ago, when Del and Phyllis felt so isolated, they could hardly imagine that they would one day attend the Gay Games and see lesbians elected to public office and appointed as judges.

"Heavens, no! We get excited when all these things happen! That keeps us going. We've seen so much change. We know it can happen. Certainly, what has happened in our lifetime was not expected by us. What happens is that these small successes spur you on. And we never burn out!" smiles Del.

"By the time we found out about burn-out, I think that it was too late! We just continued being active! Recently, people have been calling us 'doyennes.' I haven't figured out what that means exactly!" laughs Phyllis.

"We wouldn't have stayed in the movement if it hadn't been fun," says Del.

T HEY OFTEN FEEL THEY ARE ADMIRED more for the longevity of their relationship than their political work, which mystifies them. They don't have any special secrets for staying together.

"If we knew that, if we had this magic potion or whatever, we would have made a million dollars," declares Phyllis.

But Del credits their "solid friendship" and compatibility.

"I would sort of get out on a limb—and Phyllis would come along to pick up the pieces and smooth things over."

"We are a good match," agrees Phyllis. "This sounds kind of strange, but I think that we did start out with the idea that we were getting together for good, which is what the idea of marriage was. Although we didn't exactly call ourselves married—we're talking about the fifties—we came out of a middle-class tradition. The idea was that you stayed together come hell or high water. I don't think that we knew any more than anybody else did. We just said we were going to do it. And it turned out that we were right."

"We just started out with an assumption," says Del.

"I don't think anybody ever knows. We were very fortunate. We wanted to do the same thing. I mean—what if she had been a Republican?" Phyllis questions with a laugh.

As their shared laughter dies down, Phyllis continues thoughtfully, "You need to love the person. Warts and all. If you don't do that, you're in deep doo-doo."

"And," adds Del, "just because you have an argument or something, it isn't the end of the world."

T HE LATEST THING THAT DEL AND PHYLLIS want to do together is educate people about growing old. They were recently appointed to the White House Conference on Aging. Of 2,217 delegates, only three were out lesbians, yet they managed to get sexual orientation on the agenda.

"We thought there ought to be some gay and lesbian input into this thing—because there are gay and lesbian elders," says Phyllis. "Our age is a very closeted age group."

"They've been closeted all their lives," Del adds. "And it is very difficult to advocate for an invisible constituency."

They are now involved with Old Lesbians Organizing for Change.

"We are trying to make 'old' a positive word," explains Del.

"Getting old is much better than the other option, which is to die!" Phyllis laughs.

"So what we are up against is ageism! We've lived through homophobia and sexism. Now we are living through ageism, and it is quite a challenge. But I think the thing that was part of our being so involved in the movement was the challenge.

"Being active in your old age is healthy—physically, mentally, and emotionally. Some men who retire don't know what to do with themselves. And we can't believe it! We're as busy or busier today than back in the days when we were working! I may be older in years, but that doesn't mean I have lost my wits," Del declares with a grin.

"The white hair gets 'em every time!" laughs Phyllis.

Cecelia Hayden-Smith & Esther Smith

ESTHER SMITH AND CECELIA HAYDEN-SMITH FIRST met—and first kissed—in this dining room.

"She was a fast hussy!" laughs Esther, remembering that day ten years ago, when Cecelia catered a wedding reception at her house. Photos were being snapped, and a guest had yelled, "Somebody do something!" So Cecelia did.

"I just grabbed Esther and kissed her. Then, I thought, 'Oh my God, what did I do? This woman is going to think I am a horrible person.' So I apologized, and she said, 'Well, ya know, it was okay. I could stand some more of that.'"

"There was something I did like about her," continues Esther. "She had a beautiful smile for one thing, and she looks good walking away, I tell you! Then when we finally danced, she just fit right in my arms. I saw a lot in Cecelia that she didn't see. I had prayed and asked God—I had a list of things that I wanted, and she's just about all those things! She's a lot of fun. She makes life interesting. She talks a lot—and I'm quiet—so she keeps something going all the time. She's got a heart as big as all outdoors."

"Gosh, I just love my Boo," sighs Cecelia, giving Esther's hand a squeeze. "When I get flustered, she takes care of me. I love the way that she just knows when I need a hug or some space. I love her for the fact that she loves me unconditionally and she respects and honors me. I've been much bigger than this and I've been a lot thinner than this, but I haven't been happier than this."

At one point in her life Cecelia weighed nearly five hundred pounds. "You eat because you are stuffing things you don't want to deal with. I felt bad about myself. I felt something was wrong with me.

"I always had feelings for women. I come from such a tiny town in rural Maryland that I didn't know any gay people. The one or two that I heard of were treated so horribly. So the feelings I had I buried them really, really deep."

When she was eighteen she moved to D.C. and three years later had a son, Darryl, who she raised alone. "He is the delight of my life!" Cecelia worked several jobs at once to be able to afford private school for Darryl. It was only once he finished school that he realized they had ever been poor.

It wasn't until he was a grown man that Cecelia decided to come out. "I thought I was the only black, almost forty-year-old lesbian trying to come out in D.C.! I went to a workshop on 'coming-out after forty'—there must have been fifty women there, but I was the only black woman in that room. I came out kickin' and screamin' but I never felt more comfortable in my life. It just felt so good the first time I gave myself permission to look at a woman sexually. That was such a freeing thing for me. I was ready to date all the women in Maryland, Washington, Virginia! I was just beginning to really, really have fun. And that's when I met Esther!"

ESTHER GREW UP DURING THE DEPRESSION, the only girl in a family of six boys. "I was a tomboy, always climbing and wrestling and fighting. I had quite a temper. When I came out 'into the life,' my church didn't like that very much, so they asked me to leave. I did, but I knew within myself that no matter where I went, God was still with me. Soon afterward I found out about the Metropolitan Community Church. Now I'm a deacon, and I sing in the Gospel Choir!"

In 1953, Esther's family moved to the house where Esther grew up and where Cecelia and Esther "began courting." And it was also where they decided to marry.

"This is a special house that Esther and I have created together," says Cecelia. "It's made out of brick and mortar with love that cements it. We attribute that to our relationship and to Jesus Christ, who is the center of our lives."

Every year three to four hundred people come to Esther and Cecelia's house on Christmas Day. "In our community, a lot of people don't have homes to go to. They don't have loving parents who care about them. People who don't have places to go know that they can come here. They know there is going to be enough food and enough

love. Everybody's welcome—straight, gay, old people, babies, and every kind of nationality. God blessed me, I am a wonderful cook," Cecelia beams with pride. "They call the dining room Around-the-World-with-Cecelia's-Cookin'! I make more than fifty pies and cakes. I make stuffed duck with wild rice, lamb, ham, turkey, lasagna, homemade rolls, cornbread. . . . It takes me a week to make all of it.

"Esther and I want people to know that lesbians can be together a really long time, you can have wonderful friends, your family can be supportive of you. I wish and I pray before I die that more people would come out, and not live a lie. The Christian Right is not right! They interpret God's word to make this a very hateful, scared country. They prey on gays and lesbians because they always have to have someone beneath them to make themselves feel good, but as far as I am concerned they have no power over me. We know that God made us, and God doesn't make mistakes. People have no reason to fear us or to want to hurt us. We are living our lives as God would have us be."

WHEN CECELIA AND ESTHER knew they wanted to live their lives together, forever, they decided to marry. "I had never been married," Cecelia muses, "and I wanted my dream wedding. I didn't care that it wasn't going to be legal in front of Gingrich or somebody. Who cares about him? I asked Esther if we could have it, and she said yes."

They saved for two years to pay for it. "I can't tell you how much it cost, you'll think we're crazy," Esther laughs.

Cecelia, in planning their wedding, also planned to come out to her grown son.

"You can keep your lesbian life a secret as long as you don't have nobody special. I wanted to spend the rest of my life with Esther and, you know, you can't hide the rest of your life."

Cecelia told him when he was home on leave from the service. It didn't go well.

"Oh my poor mother's heart! It was just broke because my baby was never going to speak to me again. I just fell to pieces. I boo-hooed and carried on, but I didn't do it in front of him. I almost died, but I held my ground. What I said to him was, 'Darryl, it's time that I not lie to you or nobody else. I will never lie to anybody about my sexuality again as long as I live. I am a lesbian. There will never be a man in my life. I know you don't necessarily like this. You can carry on all you want. But I am your mother. You cannot take that away from me. And you are not going to disrespect me . . . ever!'"

Darryl stormed out that day and later returned for visits—with only grudging civility.

"He wouldn't halfway speak to me," says Esther. "But the next year, on the first Mother's Day after Cecelia told him, he came in the bedroom and said, 'I'm getting ready to go, Ma.' He leaned down and kissed her, and then he came over on the other side and kissed *me* goodbye! I thought I'd black out!"

On December 29, 1990, when Esther and Cecelia were married in front of three hundred and twenty-six guests, it was Darryl who walked Cecelia down the aisle.